Crane's Blue Book of Stationery

Crane's Blue Book of Stationery

THE STYLES AND ETIQUETTE OF LETTERS, NOTES, AND INVITATIONS

edited by
STEVEN L. FEINBERG

DOUBLEDAY
New York London Toronto Sydney Auckland

Common sense and consideration should be the
basis of etiquette and good manners.

John Quincy Adams

Published by Doubleday, a division of
Bantam Doubleday Dell Publishing Group, Inc.
666 Fifth Avenue, New York, New York 10103

Doubleday and the portrayal of an anchor
with a dolphin are trademarks of
Doubleday, a division of Bantam Doubleday Dell
Publishing Group, Inc.

LIBRARY OF CONGRESS CATALOGING-IN-PUBLICATION DATA

Crane's blue book of stationery : the styles and etiquette of letters,
notes, and invitations / edited by Steven L. Feinberg. — 1st ed.
    p. cm.
    Includes index.
    1. Social stationery.   I. Feinberg, Steven L.   II. Crane (Firm)
III. Title: Crane's bluebook of stationery.
BJ2081.C74   1989   88-37236
395'.4—dc19   CIP
ISBN 0-385-26175-6 (HARDCOVER)
0-385-26260-4 (SPECIAL EDITION)
Copyright © 1989 by Crane & Co., Inc.

All Rights Reserved
Printed in the United States of America
August 1989
FG
First Edition

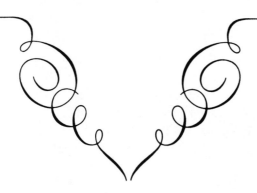

FOREWORD

From the beginning of recorded history, man has had a need for a final arbiter of his modes and manners. In several chapters of the Bible, there are instances of this practice, as in the book of Leviticus, the book of Proverbs, and the Beatitudes in the book of Matthew. Finally, of course, in Exodus, there are the definitive rules of conduct, the Ten Commandments.

In the seventeenth and eighteenth centuries, numerous books of conduct were published for the edification of the young. These were primarily concerned with the subjects of good manners and proper conduct.

Richard Brathwaite wrote a provocative volume in the seventeenth century entitled *The English Gentleman & Description of a Good Wife.* According to Arthur M. Schlesinger in his *Learning How to Behave,* there is a suggestion that this book accompanied some of the colonists on the *Mayflower.* George Washington wrote his own set of standards in 1747, which he called *Rules of Civility.*

There were a series of popular books on the subject in the seventeenth and eighteenth centuries: *The Whole Duty of Man* by Richard Allestree, published in London in 1658; and *The School of Good Manners* by Eleazar Moody, published in America, which was an adaptation of the English version of a French original. Probably the best known of the eighteenth-century guides was Lord Chester-field's *Letters to His Son*.

Then in the twentieth century, the most renowned name in etiquette became Emily Post, whose *Etiquette* was the standard work for fifty years. It was first published in 1922 and went through fourteen editions. Following her death, the mantle was assumed by Amy Vanderblit, and subsequently by Millicent Fenwick, who edited *Vogue's Book of Etiquette*. In the past few years, the dictator of social usage has been Judith Martin's *Miss Manners' Guide to Excruciatingly Correct Behavior*. Most of these authors have been self-appointed arbiters with only casual credentials for their authority and, at times, pontifical dicta.

Crane, a manufacturer of top-quality social stationery since 1801, has met and solved virtually every problem of correct usage in the area of written or engraved communications.

The company has been the provider of paper to all of the leading stationers in America and has stuck steadfastly to its standards of taste, style, and quality, refusing to compromise at any time for any customer. The company's devotion to quality and its unquestioned integrity led the federal government to name Crane as its source of production for the paper used in United States currency.

As a result, Crane has earned a position of respect and honor that has not been equaled by any single name in American papermaking history. Crane's authority to write this *Blue Book of Stationery* is unchallenged.

My first association with Crane occurred when I was a freshman at Amherst College in 1921. Since Dalton, Massachusetts, was not far distant, I seized the opportunity to visit the factory to learn the fundamentals of fine papermaking.

Seven years later, when I was assigned the responsibility of opening a stationery department at Neiman Marcus, I immediately went to Crane's for counsel and advice, which they gave generously and unselfishly. The standard of the department was based on Crane's quality, a relationship that has persisted for sixty years.

The management of Crane's has changed with time, but never has its sense of purpose or direction wavered; never has its quality been tampered with; never have its standards of taste succumbed to the vagaries of fashion.

The company is unique in world industry: it has a name that is without competition; almost two hundred years old, it is still going strong, with members of the founding family still active in its operation.

Stanley Marcus
Chairman Emeritus
Neiman Marcus Company
Dallas, 1988

CONTENTS

    AND SOCIAL CORRESPONDENCE   155

        Holiday Cards   157

        Jewish New Year Cards   159

        Birth Announcements   161
            Mother Uses Maiden Name   163
            Twins   163

        Adoption Announcements   164

        Christening Invitations   165

        Change of Address Announcements   166

        Change of Name Announcements   168

        Thank-You Notes   168

        Memorial Service Invitations   170

        Condolence Notes   171

        Sympathy Acknowledgments   172

6   BUSINESS AND PROFESSIONAL STATIONERY   177

        Introduction   179

        Corporate Letterhead   179

        Monarch Sheets   181

        Correspondence Cards   182

        Business Cards   184

        Social Business Cards   185

        Message Cards   186

        Business Invitations   187
            Invitation with Enclosure Card   190

        Business Announcements   192

Crane's Blue Book of Stationery

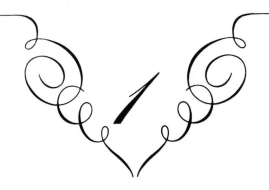

THE ESSENCE OF ETIQUETTE

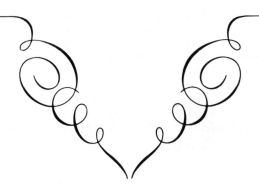

Etiquette is defined as the body of rules of social conduct that tells us what our society considers proper and acceptable behavior. These rules allow us to deal more cordially and effectively with our personal and professional relationships. Our knowledge of etiquette allows us to feel comfortable in most situations. Most of us like to know what is expected of us, and we feel more comfortable when we know we are doing what is expected of us.

A properly worded letter or invitation facilitates written communication. Social stationery etiquette, like etiquette in general, is made up of three components: Common sense, courtesy, and usage.

Etiquette's foundation is common sense. On an invitation, there is certain information that must be conveyed. Your guests need to know who is inviting them to what function. They need to know the date, time, and place. A properly worded wedding invitation contains that information and presents it coherently.

Courtesy is the spirit of etiquette. It is the ingredient that makes for more gracious and rewarding relationships. Courtesy imposes on us a consideration of others.

There are some rules of etiquette you may read about in this book and others that you feel are not right for a situation that you are in.

If you followed them, you might offend one of your parents or a stepparent. You will probably feel that your relationship with your family is more important to you than the wording of an invitation. In such a case, you may want to consider deviating from the proper wording and using a wording that does not offend anyone. Etiquette should be used to facilitate relationships, not to harm them. It is, however, important for you to know what is proper, so that if you do need to do something special you will be able to follow the rules of etiquette as closely as possible.

The third component of etiquette is usage. Our etiquette has evolved over the years and will continue to evolve. Many of the customs that were proper fifty years ago seem quaint and outdated now—a gentleman tipping his hat comes to mind. Likewise, many customs that we practice today will be outdated fifty years from now.

As old customs become obsolete, new ones are added. Through usage, new customs become a part of our etiquette. Reply cards were once considered improper, insulting, and horrendous. (Some people still feel that way.) Wedding invitations were always answered in one's own handwriting on one's own stationery. Today, the majority of wedding invitations are sent with reply cards. They are being used because they are filling a new need.

Women were once the social secretaries of the household. They had the time to properly answer their social correspondence. As women entered the workforce in large numbers, they took on new responsibilities that left them little time to properly reply to wedding invitations.

Hosts and hostesses, of course, still needed to know how many guests to expect. They did not want to guess (or make hundreds of phone calls), especially in light of the expense involved in hosting a reception. Common sense told them that, if they wanted more replies, they had better make it easier for their guests. Their answer was the reply card.

Reply cards and envelopes provide a courtesy for the guests. It is easy for them to simply check a box and mail a stamped, pre-addressed envelope. It is certainly much easier than composing a formal reply. Through usage, reply cards have become acceptable, if not proper. Our etiquette continues to change, pruning what becomes obsolete, while gradually adopting new practices to accommodate society's ever changing needs.

Paper and printing are as much a part of social stationery etiquette as the wording of invitations, announcements, and calling cards are. Paper is a commodity that we take for granted, yet it plays an important part in our lives every day. We write on it, read newspapers printed on it, and spend it when we go shopping.

Paper has been a part of civilization since the Egyptians developed a paperlike substance called "papyrus" four thousand years ago. (Our word "paper" is derived from "papyrus.") Papyrus is a reed that grows along the banks of the Nile. Called bulrushes in the Bible, they were the reeds in which Moses was hidden from Pharoah.

The papyrus plant touched Egyptian civilization at many levels. The head was used to decorate the altars of the gods, and the wood of the root was used for tools and utensils. Boats, sails, cloth, and cords were made from the stem. The soft, thin layers of the inner stem were used to make the writing surface that was the forerunner of paper.

The Egyptians shaved off the inner stem with a knife. Two shavings were pressed together and set out in the sun to dry. They dried into sheets that were smooth enough to write on.

Papyrus was exported to Greece through the Egyptian port city of Biblos. "Biblos" became the Greek word for the writings made on papyrus. Our word "bible" is derived from the Greek word "Biblos." During the early Christian era, "Biblos" came to be used to represent the most important writings made on papyrus.

Modern papermaking has its origins in China. During the first century A.D. Ts'ai Lun created the art of papermaking.

Ts'ai Lun took silk, linen, and old fish nets and placed them in stone mortars, where they were beaten to a pulp. The pulp was saturated with water, allowing its fibers to intertwine. A mold was dipped into the pulp, and a layer was removed. The mold was then set in the sun to dry. The finished product was a strong and durable sheet of paper.

The Chinese buried their dead with all their earthly possessions, encouraging grave robbers to plunder their graves in pursuit of riches. As a precaution, fake paper currency was developed to be used instead of gold and silver coins, which discouraged grave robbers from disturbing the remains of the dead. Today, some Asian societies still bury their dead with paper that represents the possessions of the deceased (paper houses and paper Rolls Royces, for example), a practice started during the early days of Chinese papermaking.

For seven centuries, the art of papermaking lay locked in China. Then, during the battle of Samarkand in the eighth century, the Arabs captured some Chinese papermakers, who, after untold torture, revealed the secrets of making paper.

Before paper became widely used in the Middle East, the Arabs used parchment as a writing material. Parchment was an animal skin that was specially tanned to give it a surface smooth enough to be written upon.

Two terms that we use today, "kid finish" and "vellum," are derived from the parchment made from the skins of young animals. Parchment made from kid or vellum was finer and more desirable. Kid and vellum papers (the words are used interchangeably now) have a soft, rich feel and are generally preferred for social invitations and correspondence.

The knowledge of papermaking entered Europe through the Arab colonies of Spain and Sicily. From these bases, it spread throughout Europe, and later to the New World.

The great advantage that paper held over papyrus and parchment was that it could be bound into books. Papyrus cracked and parchment was much too thick. Paper made from cotton fiber can last for hundreds of years, as evidenced by copies of the Gutenberg Bible, printed more than five hundred years ago, that have survived to this day in sound condition.

The first paper mill in America was built in 1690 by William Rittenhouse. Rittenhouse, who came to America as the leader of a group of Mennonites, settled in Germantown, Pennsylvania. Rittenhouse built his mill in partnership with William Bradford, public printer to the colony. Bradford used most of the mill's output for his own printing and continued to be its largest customer after his move to New York. (Bradford was asked to leave Pennsylvania by the Quaker authorities.) In New York Bradford became the official printer to the crown during the reign of King William and Queen Mary. He printed New York's first paper currency, the first American *Book of Common Prayer*, and *The Gazette*, New York's first newspaper.

Rittenhouse and other papermakers made their paper by hand from cotton and linen rags. Rag merchants purchased rags from housewives and sold them to paper mills. A humorous ditty of the time told a story about the value of rags:

Rags make paper,
Paper makes money,
Money makes banks,
Banks make loans,
Loans make beggars,
Beggars make rags.

ANONYMOUS, EIGHTEENTH CENTURY

Rags were washed, cut, and gently beaten into tiny fibers. The fibers were soaked in water and stored in a large holding tank. The pulp was transferred in smaller quantities to the vat. The vatman used a mold made of a wire screen and a wooden frame to remove the pulp. The frame is called the deckle, and that is where the term "deckle paper" comes from. Deckle papers are papers with unfinished edges.

The vatman dipped the mold into the vat, flipped the excess pulp from the mold, and shook the mold to remove excess water. The partially dried sheet was removed from the mold and stacked with other sheets. The sheets were pressed to squeeze more water from them and then were taken to a loft where they were hung, allowing them to dry completely.

The second half of the nineteenth century saw a new technology developed to produce paper from wood pulp instead of cotton. Many manufacturers took advantage of this technology and produced lower quality, less expensive paper. You have probably read stories about how books in the Library of Congress and our local libraries are decomposing and rotting away. This is of great concern to historians and librarians. The problem stems from the fact that the paper used in these books is made of wood pulp. Acid is used to break wood down into a pulp. The acid continues to work in the paper, causing it to decompose.

Cotton fibers used in papermaking can be broken down through gentle beating and refining. No harsh acids are used that would cause the paper to decompose prematurely. Wedding invitations and social stationery made from 100-percent cotton fiber will last for years, preserving your memories.

Cotton-fiber paper is still made the same way it was made almost two thousand years ago by Ts'ai Lun. State-of-the-art equipment performs many of the functions that were once performed by men and women, but the process itself remains the same.

Cotton arrives from southern cotton fields in a crudely processed form. Rags are rarely used now, so the term "rag paper" is really a misnomer, although rag paper has come to mean paper made from 100-percent cotton fiber.

The cotton is placed in washers where it is cleaned and soaked. The mixture moves to the beaters, where it is shredded into a pulp of tiny fibers. If a colored paper such as ecru is being made, the die is added during this stage. The pulp goes through a final cleansing and onto the papermaking machine. (The machine that Crane and Co. uses to make their social and wedding papers is 175 feet long.)

The pulp is 99-percent water when it enters the machine. The machine's job is to remove the water, transforming the pulp into paper. The pulp is spread out over a vibrating screen. Water is suctioned off as the pulp moves along the screen. Halfway down the screen, the watermark is applied to the paper by a dandy roll. A watermark is an impression made in the paper that can be seen when you hold it up to the light. A dandy roll is a wire cylinder on which is soldered whatever impression is going to be made in the paper. The dandy roll rotates, and the watermark is impressed into the pulp when it is still more than half water. The pulp leaves the screen and enters the driers as a wet web of paper.

The driers cook the water out of the paper. External sizing is added to give the paper a surface that can be written on without blotting. At one time, sizing was made from the hides of water buffalo.

The paper leaves the papermaking machine and is wound into huge rolls. The paper is cut into flat sheets (generally about 21" x 33") that are then inspected. The sheets that pass inspection are converted into stationery. Envelopes are lined and folded; sheets are trimmed and, perhaps, bordered by hand, tied with a ribbon, and assembled and packaged carefully. All of this, before the consumer even sees it.

Once you have selected an appropriate paper for your stationery, you will need to decide how to personalize it. There are two processes from which to choose: engraving and thermography. Engraving is the finer of the two—its lines are much sharper and more distinct than those formed by thermography.

Centuries ago, official documents and announcements were penned by hand in monastic schools. The introduction of engraving in the mid-seventeenth century made it possible to reproduce this beautiful handwriting. Many of the engraving styles available today can be traced back to those early calligraphic styles.

The beauty of engraving lies in the contrasting thick and thin lines and in its three-dimensional quality. When you are at your stationer, look closely at an engraved invitation. You will see that, while all of the copy is raised, some lines are raised more than others. Heavy lines are etched deeper into the engraving plate, so the raise is more pronounced. Thin lines are more delicate. The paper is not raised as much, and the effect is a fine, sharp line. No other process is capable of producing this multilevel effect.

Engraving was once done solely by hand. An engraver cut an image in reverse into a copper plate or steel die by hand. Today, some engraving is still done by hand, but a modern method called photoengraving is now commonly used.

The first step in the photoengraving process is composition. Using state-of-the-art equipment, the copy is put on film in the appropriate lettering style. The film is then stripped and set up in the desired layout.

The film is placed on a chemically treated copper plate. Light, passing through the film, exposes the surface of the plate. The plate is then dipped in acid and the unexposed surface is etched.

The die is now ready to be die-stamped. Die-stamping is the process of transferring ink to paper from an engraving die.

The die is placed on the press, and a cardboard counter is cut to approximately the size of the area taken up by the engraved letters on the die. The counter concentrates the pressure of the press on the part of the paper that is to be inked. It forces the paper into the cavity of the die.

On the press, ink is applied to the die. The ink is wiped off the surface of the die but remains in the engraved cavity. The counter forces the paper into the cavity and raises the surface of the paper. The ink adheres to the raised surface. It is this third dimension that creates the sharp definition associated with the engraving process.

Thermography, sometimes called raised printing, is a process that also creates a raised image. Although not as fine as engraving, thermography creates its raised image without a copper plate.

Like engraving, the process begins in composition. There, the copy is set on film in the appropriate lettering style. The copy is stripped and set up in the appropriate layout. Instead of a copper plate, a paper plate with an aluminum backing is created. This plate has the capacity to chemically transfer the image of the copy to the paper.

The plate is mounted on a cylinder on the press. It comes in contact with wetting rollers and then with ink rollers. The ink is offset onto a blanket cylinder. The paper picks up the image as it passes between the blanket cylinder and the impression cylinder. The copy is flat-printed on the paper.

While the ink is still wet, it is dusted with a resinous powder. Some of the powder sticks to the inked impression. The excess powder is vacuumed from the surface before the paper passes through a heated tunnel. The heat melts the powder, which forms a clear, raised surface over the printed image. The paper itself remains flat. It is the powder that creates the raised effect.

You can tell the difference between engraving and thermography (raised printing) in one of three ways: (1) The inks used in thermography are much shinier than engraving inks. (2) Engraving creates an indentation in the back of the paper. This is caused by the pressure of the die press forcing the paper into the cavity of the plate. This pressure causes the paper to be raised and creates the sharp, distinctive lines that are associated with engraving. (3) Engraving creates a bruise on the front of the paper. If you look very closely at the area around the copy, you will notice that the paper surrounding the copy is slightly smoother than the rest of the paper. The smoothness is created by the pressure exerted by the die. The pressure smooths out the paper in the same way an iron presses a cotton shirt.

The indentation and the bruise are desirable. Many people look for these indications to see if stationery is engraved.

Proper social correspondence results from using the correct paper, printing process, and etiquette. All three should play an important role in your choice of stationery and invitations that are appropriate for you, while conforming to the standards of etiquette.

SOCIAL
STATIONERY

THE SOCIAL STATIONERY WARDROBE

A stationery wardrobe can consist of any number of different papers. It may seem to you that there is a special paper for every letter that you write. However, while there are many different types of paper from which to choose, you may start out with just two: one for writing notes and one for writing letters.

As with the clothes you wear, the stationery you use makes a statement about you. Therefore, you should always use a high-quality paper for your personal stationery. Papers made from 100-percent cotton fiber are the best.

Your stationery can be either engraved with a copper plate, printed in thermography, or flat-printed. Engraving offers you the most elegant look, and, while engraving is initially more expensive than the other processes, its look is much more appealing. Most of the additional cost of engraving is in the initial process of cutting the die, which can be used over and over again.

Thermography, or raised printing, offers a look that is similar to, but not as fine as, engraving. While engraving your stationery will give you a finer look, you may wish to print some of your stationery in thermography.

Your name or monogram may appear on your stationery. As letters are written by only one person, only one person's name or monogram properly appears on stationery.

Social Papers for Women

Letter Sheets

Letter sheets are the most formal papers in a woman's stationery wardrobe. They are ecru or white and have a fold along the left-hand side. (Formal wedding invitations are engraved on letter sheets.) The letter sheet folds again from top to bottom to fit inside an envelope that is approximately half its size.

Blank, unadorned letter sheets are used to reply to formal invitations and for letters of condolence. Because of their simplicity and elegance, letter sheets may be used for any type of correspondence.

Letter sheets may be adorned with an engraved or blind embossed coat of arms or monogram. They may also be engraved with an address for use as house stationery.

One writes on pages 1, 3, and 2 of a letter sheet, in that order. The back page of a letter sheet is never written on.

Monogrammed Notes

Monograms were created hundreds of years ago as a way for illiterate members of royalty to authorize documents and proclamations. Charlemagne was one of the early users of monograms. He was unable to write his name, so he drew his monogram in lieu of signing his name.

Women use monogrammed notes to write thank-you notes, to extend formal invitations, and to send short messages to friends and acquaintances. You should choose a monogram style that reflects your taste and personality. If you choose to have your notes engraved, you will need to purchase an engraving die. Your engraving die can be used again and again, so you should choose a lettering style that has lasting appeal.

Notes start on page 1 when the monogram is engraved at the top of the note. The note continues to page 3, then to page 2, if absolutely necessary. When the monogram is engraved in the center of the note, the note is written on page 3. You cannot use page 2, since the engraving on page 1 causes an indentation on page 2.

The correct initials for married women to use are those representing her first name, maiden name, and married name. When all of the letters in the monograms are the same size, the initials appear in order. Many monogram styles have a larger center initial. In these styles, the initial representing the woman's married name appears in the middle, flanked by the initials of her given and maiden names.

Single women and married women who retain their maiden name use the initials representing their first, middle, and last names. They appear in order in monogram styles in which all of the letters are the same size. When using a monogram style in which the middle initial is larger, the initial of the surname appears in the middle, flanked by the initials of the given name.

MARRIED WOMAN

(Nina Spooner Johnson)

SINGLE WOMAN

(Kathleen Anne Crater)

Informals

Contrary to their name, informals are rather formal. They are small white or ecru foldover notes that are usually the smallest allowable mailing size. They are engraved in black ink and may have a blind embossed frame.

Informals are engraved with a woman's proper social name, preceded by her title. "Mr. and Mrs." is properly used on informals only when they are used to issue an informal invitation from both husband and wife.

Informals are used to issue informal invitations, to respond to informal invitations, to send very brief messages, and as gift enclosures. They are not properly used as calling cards or thank-you notes.

You usually write on page 3 of an informal but when sending brief messages or invitations, you may write on the front.

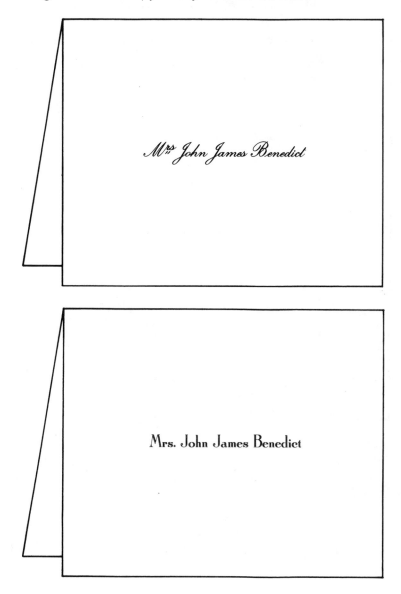

Message Cards

Message cards are single cards, large enough to mail, that are used for greetings, informal invitations, and replies to informal invitations. Message cards are ecru or white and are engraved in black ink.

A woman's full social name, preceded by her title, appears near the top center of the card, with the address (only the street address in a large city; street address, city, and state in a small town) in the top right-hand corner.

1040 Fifth Avenue

Mrs. Martin Merrimac MacDonald

47 Clapboard Ridge
Greenwich, Connecticut

Mrs. Clayton Phillip O'Henry

Half Sheets

Half sheets were originally called half sheets because they were half the size of formal letter sheets. Half sheets are single sheets of paper that fold in half to fit their envelopes. They may be embellished with a monogram, a name, an address, a name and address, or a coat of arms. Half sheets and monogrammed notes can be ordered to match.

Only the front of the half sheet is written on, never the back. When more space is needed, an unembellished second sheet is used.

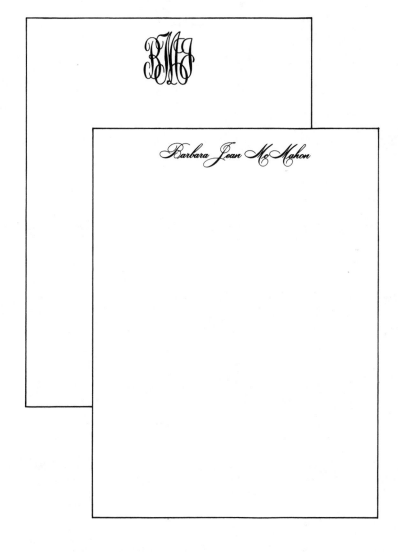

Correspondence Cards

One of the most useful items in a stationery wardrobe is a correspondence card. More informal than a note, these cards are used for thank-yous, informal invitations, and short notes.

Correspondence cards are flat, heavy cards that are mailed in their corresponding envelopes. They can be plain or bordered, depending on one's tastes.

A name, a monogram, or a coat of arms may appear at the top of the card. One writes only on the front of the card.

Helen Jane Nicholson

Monarch Sheets

Although not used very often by a woman, a monarch sheet can be used for long letters or personal business letters. A monarch sheet measures 7¼" x 10½" and folds twice to fit its envelope.

A woman's name, address, or name and address appear at the top of the sheet. Although not incorrect, a monogram is not generally used on a monarch sheet.

Only the front of the sheet is written on, never the back. If additional space is needed, blank second sheets are used.

Rhonda Sue Burke
9229 Sunset Boulevard
Los Angeles, California 90064

9229 Sunset Boulevard
Los Angeles, California 90064

Rhonda Sue Burke

Postcards

Postcards can be engraved with either the name or the name and address on one line at the top of the card. They are used for simple, nonconfidential correspondence. The maximum size that the Postal Service accepts for reduced rate postage is 4" x 6".

House Stationery

House stationery may properly be used by any resident of the house or by any guest staying at that address. Many people order house stationery for their country homes so that engraved stationery is always available for their guests. House stationery may show the name of the house or estate, or simply the address.

4010 Raquet Street
Nacodoches, Texas 75961

Green Meadow Farm

Envelopes

The return address should always appear on the flap of an envelope used with social stationery. The use of the name with the address is proper, but it is more elegant to show just the address. When the address is in an apartment building, the name or the apartment number should appear with the address. (The nine-digit Zip Code, customarily used in business, may also be used on personal stationery.)

2319 Princess Ann Street
Greensboro, North Carolina 27408

Apartment 25 J
180 East End Avenue
New York, New York 10028

180 East End Avenue, Apt. 25 J
New York, New York 10028

Social Papers for Men

Monarch Sheets

Most men use monarch sheets (7¼" x 10½") for their personal letters and personal business letters. Monarch sheets fold twice to fit their envelopes. Although monarch sheets are available in a variety of colors, most men prefer ecru and white. Many different ink colors are also available, but most men choose black, grey, or navy blue.

Men put their name, address, or name and address at the top of the sheets. The stationery retains a more personal look when only the name is shown.

Only the front of the sheet is written on, never the back. If additional space is needed, blank second sheets are used.

MICHAEL SCAGLUSO

3930 BISSONNET

HOUSTON, TEXAS 77005

MICHAEL SCAGLUSO

3930 BISSONNET

HOUSTON, TEXAS 77005

Half Sheets

Men who usually do not write long letters may prefer half sheets to monarch sheets. Half sheets are smaller than monarch sheets and fold in half to fit their envelopes. They may be embellished with a coat of arms or a monogram, but most men prefer to show just their names.

Like the monarch sheets, only the front of a half sheet is written on, never the back. Blank second sheets are used when more space is needed.

MICHAEL SCAGLUSO

Correspondence Cards

Correspondence cards are used for thank-you notes and brief correspondence. Men should use them instead of foldover notes. Foldover notes are small notes that fold top to bottom and should only be used by women.

The cards are very practical, and many men find they use more correspondence cards than sheets. Usually, a name or monogram appears at the top, although you might want to put your name and address on one line across the top. Only the front of the card is written on.

MJS

MICHAEL SCAGLUSO

MICHAEL SCAGLUSO · 3930 BISSONNET · HOUSTON, TEXAS 77005

Envelopes

Envelopes for social stationery are imprinted with the address on the back flap. The name can be shown but is usually omitted. If an address is in an apartment building, the name or the apartment number should be shown. (The nine-digit Zip Code, customarily used in business, may also be used on personal stationery.)

MICHAEL SCAGLUSO
3930 BISSONNET
HOUSTON, TEXAS 77005

3930 BISSONNET, APT. 324
HOUSTON, TEXAS 77005

3930 BISSONNET • 324
HOUSTON, TEXAS 77005

25

INVITATIONS TO
SOCIAL OCCASIONS

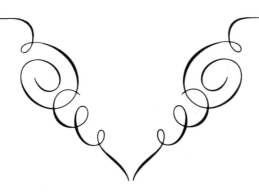

INTRODUCTION

*I*nvitations to social occasions may be formal or informal. The style of the invitation should match the formality (or informality) of the event.

If the event is not formal, more freedom is allowed in designing the invitation. The invitations may be done on a correspondence card with a bright colored border and a matching lined envelope. The lettering style may be fun and frivolous. This is a chance to be as creative as your imagination allows.

The composition for all invitations contains the same basic elements. While the rules for an informal invitation are much looser than those for a formal invitation, the same information must be proffered.

An invitation with a formal composition is shown and diagramed on the following page. It is followed by an invitation to the same event with an informal composition. Notice that, although the presentation is different, the same information is given.

Mr and Mrs Stephen Julian Hameroff
INVITATIONAL LINE

request the pleasure of your company
REQUEST LINE

for cocktails and dinner
EVENT LINE

Thursday, the fifteenth of June
DATE LINE

at seven o'clock
TIME LINE

2126 Lazy Lane
LOCATION LINE

Houston, Texas
CITY AND STATE LINE

The favour of a reply is requested
REPLY REQUEST LINE

—————

You are cordially invited
REQUEST LINE

for cocktails and dinner
EVENT LINE

on Thursday, June 15th
DATE LINE

at 7 o'clock
TIME LINE

2126 Lazy Lane
LOCATION LINE

Houston, Texas
CITY AND STATE LINE

Janet and Steve Hameroff
INVITATIONAL LINE

Please reply
(713) 555-1212
REPLY REQUEST LINE

30

Formal Dinner

Formal dinner invitations are properly engraved on ecru or white letter sheets. Black ink should be used.

Correspondence cards are sometimes used instead of letter sheets, but they are considered less formal. Black ink is the most formal color, but any conservative ink color engraved on a light-colored card will make a tasteful invitation.

Mr. and Mrs. Jeffrey Harris Atkinson

request the pleasure of the company of

Mr. and Mrs. Charles Winn Montgomery

at dinner

Friday, the eighteenth of November

at eight o'clock

922 Club Creek

Grosse Pointe Farms, Michigan

Mr. and Mrs. Jeffrey Harris Atkinson

request the pleasure of your company

at dinner

Friday, the eighteenth of November

at eight o'clock

922 Club Creek

Grosse Pointe Farms, Michigan

Dinner to Honor a Guest

The name of the honored guest may be presented either at the top of the invitation or in the body of the invitation.

IN HONOUR OF

ADMIRAL WILLIAM STANTON TAGG

MR. AND MRS. ARTHUR DAVID LINCOLN

REQUEST THE PLEASURE OF YOUR COMPANY

AT DINNER

THURSDAY, THE TENTH OF OCTOBER

AT EIGHT O'CLOCK

1825 SYCAMORE LANE

CHARLESTON, SOUTH CAROLINA

Mr. and Mrs. Arthur David Lincoln

request the pleasure of your company

at a dinner in honour of

Admiral William Stanton Tagg

Thursday, the tenth of October

at eight o'clock

1825 Sycamore Lane

Charleston, South Carolina

Dinner
in honor of
The Right Honorable
Winston S. Churchill
O.M., C.H., M.P.
given by
Mr. Henry R. Luce
on Friday, the twenty-fifth of March
Nineteen hundred and forty-nine
Ritz Carlton
New York

Invitations to Meet a Guest

Invitations to meet a guest are extended when the hosts wish to introduce someone to their invited guests. The invitation might be to meet a celebrity, someone new in the area, or a daughter's fiance. The format follows that of an invitation to honor a guest.

To Meet

Miss Kimberly Ann Keleher

Mr. and Mrs. Peter Thomas Madison

request the pleasure of your company

for cocktails

Wednesday, the second of April

at seven o'clock

4209 Granada Boulevard

Coral Gables, Florida

Official Invitations

Invitations issued by government officials are engraved in black ink on white or ecru cards and letter sheets.

The Vice President and Mrs. Bailey

request the pleasure of the company of

Mr. and Mrs. John Livingston

at a reception in honor of

Miss Sandra Jean Atkins

Wednesday, the third of May

from five until seven o'clock

Blair House

Diplomatic Invitations

Events hosted by, or in honor of, a foreign dignitary require properly worded invitations. If the event is in honor of a dignitary, "In honour of" or "In honor of" appears at the top of the invitation. The dignitary's title must be presented properly. It is best to check with the etiquette office of the appropriate consulate to ascertain correct titles.

To have the honour to meet
Their Majesties
The King and Queen of Siam

The Governor of Hawaii
requests the pleasure of your company
at luncheon
at Washington Place
Thursday, September seventeenth
at one o'clock

BY COMMAND OF HER MAJESTY THE QUEEN

THE NETHERLANDS AMBASSADOR

REQUESTS THE HONOR OF THE PRESENCE OF

Mr. Nicholas Chaney Worth

AT DINNER

ON THURSDAY, THE SIXTH OF AUGUST

AT EIGHT O'CLOCK

2325 FIFTEENTH STREET

In honor of

Their Britannic Majesties

The United States New York World's Fair Commission

requests the pleasure of your company

at luncheon

Saturday, the tenth of June

at one o'clock

The Federal Building

New York World's Fair

This card must be shown at the door

In honour of Their Royal Highnesses
The Princess Elizabeth, Duchess of Edinburgh and The Duke of Edinburgh

The British Ambassador and Lady Franks
request the pleasure of the company of

at a Reception
on Thursday, November 1st from 3:30 to 5:30 o'clock
at the
British Embassy

Day Clothes or Uniform

Please reply to the
Private Secretary

Party Invitations

Informal party invitations reflect the nature of the event. They can be festive, lighthearted, or conservative. Samples of informal party invitations are shown, but you should not feel restricted to any of these wordings or formats.

Joyce and Charles Fedden

invite you for cocktails

on Thursday, January 10th

at seven o'clock

333 Edgewood Road

High Point, North Carolina

GENERAL AND MRS. GORDON ALEXANDER GRANGER

REQUEST THE PLEASURE OF THE COMPANY OF

Mr. and Mrs. Chester Williston Harris

AT DINNER

TUESDAY, THE SECOND OF APRIL

AT SEVEN O'CLOCK

HOTEL THAYER

WEST POINT, NEW YORK

Lisa and Barry Garrett
cordially invite you
for dinner and dancing
Saturday, July tenth
at eight o'clock
aboard the Sea Breeze
Larchmont Yacht Club
Larchmont, New York

———————

MARIE AND CHRIS FORBES

INVITE YOU TO JOIN THEM FOR A

NEW ENGLAND CLAMBAKE

SUNDAY, THE TWELFTH OF JULY

AT TWO O'CLOCK

157 COVE ROAD

FALMOUTH, MASSACHUSETTS

———————

YOU ARE CORDIALLY INVITED
TO A DINNER
FOR BILL SPENCER
TO CELEBRATE HIS 40TH BIRTHDAY
ON FRIDAY, SEPTEMBER 12TH
AT 7 O'CLOCK
WINDSOR YACHT CLUB

CINDY SPENCER

The Directors and Officers
of the
Golden Gate Bridge and Highway District
cordially invite

to attend the ceremonies in connection
with the opening of the
Golden Gate Bridge
to traffic, on May 28, 1937, at ten o'clock A. M.
at Crissy Field
Presidio of San Francisco

R. S. V. P.

Directors		*Engineers*
William P. Filmer, Pres.	John P. McLaughlin	Joseph B. Strauss, Chief Engineer
R. H. Trumbull, Vice-Pres.	Joseph A. McMinn	*Consulting Engineers*
Arthur M. Brown, Jr.	Hugo D. Newhouse	O. H. Ammann
Frank P. Doyle	A. R. O'Brien	Leon S. Moisseiff
William D. Hadeler	Warren Shannon	Chas. Derleth, Jr.
Harry Lutgens	Richard J. Welch	*Officers*
Thomas Maxwell	Henry Westbrook, Jr.	James Reed, General Manager
		W. W. Felt, Jr. Secretary
		George H. Harlan, Attorney
		Roy S. West, Attorney

Dance Invitations

Dance invitations follow the same format as any formal invitation. The word "Dancing" appears in the lower right-hand corner.

Mr. and Mrs. Stephen James McGee

request the pleasure of your company

Saturday evening, the sixth of November

at ten o'clock

The Pierre

New York

R.s.v.p.
1040 Fifth Avenue
New York, New York 10028   *Dancing*

Invitation to a Luncheon

An invitation to a luncheon is usually engraved in black ink on a white or ecru card or letter sheet.

IN HONOUR OF

DR. HILTON GARRISON CRENSHAW

MR. AND MRS. JAMES GORDON HARRIS

REQUEST THE PLEASURE OF YOUR COMPANY

AT LUNCHEON

TUESDAY, THE TENTH OF MAY

AT TWELVE O'CLOCK

THE BROWN PALACE HOTEL

DENVER, COLORADO

Invitation to a Tea

An invitation to a tea may be extended as an engraved invitation. The words "At Home" are used to indicate an afternoon tea.

Mrs. John Leland Kensington

At Home

Tuesday, the thirteenth of September

from four until six o'clock

1776 Stone Drive

Birmingham, Alabama

Wedding Anniversaries

Invitations to a wedding anniversary celebration may be extended by the children of the couple, friends of the couple, or by the couple themselves. The marriage year and the anniversary year may appear at the top of the invitations. A joint monogram may also appear at the top, between the years.

Invitations for a fiftieth wedding anniversary may be engraved in gold, twenty-fifth anniversary invitations, in silver. Since some metallic inks may be difficult to read in certain typestyles, you may prefer to engrave the dates in gold or silver and the copy in black.

Since many couples celebrating their twenty-fifth and fiftieth wedding anniversaries already have more knickknacks than they need, it is permissable to add a line in the lower right-hand corner of the invitation reading "No gifts, please." A card may be enclosed instead, reading "Your presence is the only gift that we request."

1945   ⚜   1995

Mr. and Mrs. George Bentley Farrell, Jr.

Mr. and Mrs. Clarkson David Kent

request the pleasure of your company

at a dinner in honour of

the Fiftieth Wedding Anniversary of

Mr. and Mrs. George Bentley Farrell

Saturday, the seventeenth of October

at half after seven o'clock

The Saddle and Cycle Club

Chicago, Illinois

R. s. v. p.
209 East Lake Shore Drive
Chicago, Illinois 60611   No gifts, please

1970 *1995*

Mr and Mrs James Andrew Johnson
request the pleasure of your company
at a dinner to celebrate their
Twenty-fifth Wedding Anniversary
Saturday, the third of June
at seven o'clock
816 Valley Road, N. W.
Atlanta, Georgia

Bridal Showers

Invitations to a bridal shower are usually informal. They may follow a standard invitation format. Some bridal showers have a theme,

Susan Neely

cordially invites you

to a Bridal Shower

in honor of

Kathy Carlson

on Thursday, May fifteenth

at seven o'clock

17 Park Street

Andover, Massachusetts

inviting you to bring gifts to help decorate the bride's kitchen, stock her closet, or even add to her lingerie drawer. A line in the lower left-hand corner tells your guests what kind of items they should bring.

Susan Marie Neely

requests the pleasure of your company

at a Bridal Shower in honor of

Katherine Anne Carlson

Thursday, the fifteenth of May

at seven o'clock

17 Park Street

Andover, Massachusetts

Linens

Baby Showers

Baby shower invitations are usually informal. They may or may not follow the standard invitation wording.

Janet Russell

cordially invites you

to a surprise baby shower

in honour of

Margaret McQuinn

on Thursday, November 7th

at 7 o'clock

14 Briarwood Court

Philadelphia, Pennsylvania

Commencement Invitations

Commencement invitations are sent by a school or university, inviting family and friends to the graduation ceremony. A reply is usually not requested.

THE FACULTY AND GRADUATING CLASS

OF

SAINT MICHAEL'S ACADEMY

REQUEST THE PLEASURE OF YOUR COMPANY AT THEIR

ANNUAL COMMENCEMENT EXERCISES

SATURDAY, THE TWENTIETH OF JUNE

NINETEEN HUNDRED AND NINETY-FIVE

AT THREE O'CLOCK

ALUMNI AUDITORIUM

SHAKER HEIGHTS, OHIO

Debutante Invitations

A young woman is presented to society at a debutante ball. She may be presented at a private ball or along with other young women at a mass ball, or cotillion. Due to the expense of private balls, group balls have become much more popular.

There are a series of social events that lead up to the debutante ball: dinners, teas, tea-dances, and small dances (a small dance can be a dance of any size).

Dinner

A debutante dinner is a small dinner given before the ball.

Mr. and Mrs. Paul Thomas Kroeger

request the pleasure of your company

at dinner

in honour of their daughter

Miss Whitney Warner Kroeger

Friday, the fifth of December

at seven o'clock

377 Parkside Lane

Scarsdale, New York

R.s.v.p.   *Dancing*

Tea

Debutante teas are given in the afternoon. The phrase "At Home" is used to indicate that the invitation is for a tea. The tea is usually held for women of the debutante's mother's generation and older.

Mr. and Mrs. Paul Thomas Kroeger

Miss Whitney Warner Kroeger

At Home

Saturday, the sixth of November

at five o'clock

Tea-Dance

A tea-dance is held for the debutante's friends.

Mr. and Mrs. Paul Thomas Kroeger

Miss Whitney Warner Kroeger

At Home

Saturday, the sixth of November

at five o'clock

Dancing

Small Dance

A small dance is a dance of any size given to honour the debutante.

Mr. and Mrs. Paul Thomas Kroeger

request the pleasure of your company

at a small dance in honour of

Miss Whitney Warner Kroeger

Saturday, the second of December

at nine o'clock

Sleepy Hollow Country Club

Scarborough, New York

Cotillion

A cotillion is a group ball during which a number of young women debut.

The Governors of Sleepy Hollow

request the pleasure of the company of

Miss April Lee Fairbanks

at a ball

Saturday, the ninth of December

at nine o'clock

Sleepy Hollow Country Club

Scarborough, New York

Bar/Bat Mitzvah Invitations

"Bar mitzvah" or "bat mitzvah" means son of the commandments or daughter of the commandments. A bar mitzvah is a boy who, upon reaching the age of thirteen, has attained the age of religious duty and responsibility. Bar mitzvah is also the name of the ceremony that is performed to recognize maturity. A bat mitzvah or a bas mitzvah is a girl who achieves religious maturity. Bat mitzvah and bas mitzvah also refer to the ceremony.

There is no standard etiquette for bar or bat mitzvah invitations, but it should be remembered that a bar or bat mitzvah is a religious ceremony. The invitations should be tasteful and conservative, in keeping with the solemnity of the occasion.

Mr. and Mrs. Samuel Greenberg

cordially invite you to worship with them

on the occasion of the

Bar Mitzvah of their son

Steven

on Saturday, the seventh of April

at ten o'clock

Temple Beth Israel

Palm Beach

Luncheon will follow the services

Mr. and Mrs. Samuel Greenberg
request the honour of your presence
at the Bar Mitzvah of their son
Steven
Saturday, the seventh of April
at ten o'clock
Temple Beth Israel
Palm Beach

Luncheon following the services

49

Our son, Steven

will be called to the Torah as a Bar Mitzvah

Saturday, the seventh of April

at ten o'clock

Temple Beth Israel

Palm Beach

We invite you to worship with our family

on this happy occasion

and following the services to join us for luncheon

at our home

Deborah and Samuel Greenberg

Mr. and Mrs. Bertram Gurin

invite you to worship with them

when their daughter

Barbara Jean

will celebrate her Bat Mitzvah

Saturday, the twenty-third of January

at ten o'clock

Temple Emanu-el

Great Neck, New York

Luncheon following the services

Our daughter, Barbara, will read a portion of the Haftorah on the occasion of her Bat Mitzvah on Saturday, January twenty-third at ten o'clock.

We would be delighted to have you worship with us at Temple Emanu-el in Great Neck, New York. Lunch will follow the services.

Doris and Bert Gurin

Fill-in Invitations

Fill-in or skeleton invitations can be used for more than one occasion. When personalized, they show the host's and/or hostess's name and a request line followed by spaces to be filled in by hand. They may also be purchased over the counter without personalization.

Mr. and Mrs. Christopher Alan Ware

request the pleasure of your company

for *Dinner*

on *Friday, February, twenty-sixth*

at *Seven - thirty*

R. s. v. p.
(609) 555-1212

321 Springhouse Lane
Moorestown, New Jersey

51

Stephanie Ann Davies

cordially invites you

for *Luncheon*

on *Thursday, October sixteenth*

at *twelve o'clock*

Please reply
(215) 555-1212

You are invited

for *Dinner and Dancing*

on *Saturday, July fourth*

at *seven o'clock*

Susan and Bill O'Reilly

Singular Fill-in Invitations

Lindsay Wellington
requests the pleasure of the company of

Mr. Wallace Pembroke

at *Dinner and Dancing*

on *Saturday, the twentieth of December*

at *eight o'clock*

Plural Fill-in Invitations

Mr. and Mrs. Kenneth Winston
request the pleasure of the company of

Mr. and Mrs. Edward Niles

at *a summer evening*

on *Saturday, August fifteenth*

at *half-after eight o'clock*

The President and Mrs. Eisenhower

request the pleasure of the company of

at   o'clock

The President and Mrs. Reagan

request the pleasure of the company of

at luncheon

at   o'clock

Reminder Cards

Reminder cards are sent to invited guests to confirm any information regarding the event. They should be mailed so that they arrive one week before the event. They do not require a reply.

54

Reminder cards are used when invitations are sent well in advance of the event and when invitations are extended by phone. They are also sent, as a courtesy, to the guest of honor.

You may personalize the reminder cards or use fill-ins. The fill-in reminders can be personalized or purchased over the counter without personalization. A copy of the invitation with the words "To Remind" written on it and with the reply request information crossed out may also be sent as a reminder card.

This is to remind you that

Mr. and Mrs. Taylor Ashton Wells

expect you for dinner

Friday, the twenty-first of January

at eight o'clock

1220 Alta Loma Road

Los Angeles, California

To remind

Mr. and Mrs. Taylor Ashton Wells

request the pleasure of your company

at dinner

Friday, the twenty-first of January

at eight o'clock

1220 Alta Loma Road

R.s.v.p.   Los Angeles, California

This is to remind you that
Mr. and Mrs. Taylor Ashton Wells
expect you

for *Dinner*

on *Friday, the twenty-first of January,*

at *eight* o'clock

Hold-the-Date Cards

Hold-the-date cards are sent to out-of-town guests who might need advance notification of an event so that they have time to make any special arrangements. They are generally sent three to four months before the event. They ask the guest to set aside that date for your event. A formal invitation is sent at a later time.

Please hold the date of

Saturday, the third of March

for a dinner in honour of

Dr. Linda Evelyn Berthume

Mr. and Mrs. Winthrop Phillip Byerly

Replying to Formal Invitations

Invitations should be replied to within two days. Replies are handwritten in black ink on the first page of ecru or white letter sheets. The replies are written in the third person.

Acceptances repeat the event, date, and time. Regrets repeat just event and date and require a brief reason for the regret.

Invitations from the White House take precedence over other invitations. The only acceptable excuses for refusing White House invitations are illness, a death in the family, a wedding in the family, or being out of the country on that date.

Acceptances

Mr. and Mrs. Jay Albert Greschner
have the honour to accept
the kind invitation of
The President and Mrs. Washington
to dinner
on Monday, the twenty-first of April
at eight o'clock

Mr. and Mrs. Jay Albert Greschner
accept with pleasure
the kind invitation of
Mr. and Mrs. Kimbrough
to dinner
on Friday, the third of December
at seven o'clock

Regrets

Mr. and Mrs. Jay Albert Greschner
regret that because of a previous engagement
they will be unable to accept
the kind invitation of
Mr. and Mrs. Smith
to dinner
on Thursday, the first of December

Replying to Informal Invitations

Replies to informal invitations should be as formal or informal as the closeness of your relationship with the hostess dictates. A reply sent to your mother, for example, should be much less formal than one sent to somebody you have just met. If you are sending a regret, you should mention the reason. Replies should be made promptly and may be made on informals, message cards, monogrammed notes, or calling cards.

Acceptances

Mr. and Mrs. John Taylor Cooper
accept the kind invitation of
Mr. and Mrs. Bolton
to a dinner in honor of
Dr. Lorraine Nelson
on Saturday, the first of March

Regrets

Mr. and Mrs. John Taylor Cooper
regret that they will be unable
to accept the kind invitation of
Mr. and Mrs. Bolton
to a dinner in honor of
Dr. Lorraine Nelson
on Saturday, the first of March
due to a previous engagement

Informals

Accept with pleasure
for Saturday, March 1st at 7:00

MR. AND MRS. JOHN TAYLOR COOPER

or

Dear Helen,

John and I are pleased to accept your kind invitation to dinner on March first at seven o'clock. We look forward to seeing you.

Sincerely,

Marjorie

Message Cards

930 FIFTH AVENUE

MR. AND MRS. JOHN TAYLOR COOPER

Pleased to join you for dinner on Saturday, March first at seven o'clock

Looking forward to it!

Calling Cards

Regrets for March 1st

MR. AND MRS. JOHN TAYLOR COOPER

Monogrammed Notes

Dear Helen,

John and I are sorry to have to miss your dinner on Saturday, March first. We will be away on our annual trip to visit John, Jr. We hope you will understand.

Sincerely,
Marjorie

Beyond the Invitation

Whether you are entertaining at home, at a club, or in a restaurant, you can enhance your affair by using menu cards, place cards, table cards, and escort cards. Adding these finishing touches to your decorating and table setting will make your event a truly elegant affair.

Menu cards add a nice flourish to dinner parties. Your special meal is made more special when you present your guests with menu cards. Menu cards are white or ecru and are usually trimmed in gold or silver. They can be handwritten or engraved. Your personal monogram or corporate logo (if the dinner is a corporate function) can be engraved at the top of the cards. You may also use a motif such as a scallop shell for a seafood dinner or a cornucopia for a Thanksgiving feast. The menu is listed in the center of the card and the wines are listed to the left, opposite their corresponding courses. One card is usually shared by two guests, although it is entirely correct to place one at each guest's place.

Place cards are small white or ecru cards, trimmed in gold, silver, and other colors, that are placed at the table to identify seating arrangements. Folded place cards stand on their own, while flat cards may be used in holders appropriate to the table arrangements or simply set against the water glass. Like menu cards, place cards can be embellished with monograms, logos, and motifs. Your place cards should always match your menu cards. If your menu cards are engraved with a gold scallop shell, your place cards should be engraved with one, too.

Escort cards and envelopes tell your guests who they will be escorting to dinner. The gentleman's name is written on the envelope. The name of the lady he is escorting to dinner is written on the enclosed card. They are placed on a table outside the dining area.

Table cards and envelopes are helpful for small receptions and essential for large ones. Placed on a table outside the reception hall, they direct your guests to their respective tables. Your guest's name is handwritten on the envelope. The appropriate table number is written on the enclosed card.

Menu Cards

Dinner

Robert Mondavi Fumé Blanc 1979	**Striped Bass** **Fennel Mousse** **Dill Mustard Sauce**
Robert Mondavi Cabernet Sauvignon 1977	**Medallions of Veal Morel** **Cherry Tomato Sauté** **Snow Peas**
Korbel Natural	**Raspberry Bettina** **Florentine**

Demitasse

Place Cards

Mrs. Johnson

If there are two Mrs. Johnsons at the table, their husband's first names are added to the place cards.

Mrs. William Johnson

Escort Cards and Envelopes

ENVELOPE:

Mr. LaPlant

CARD:

Miss Coterill

Table Cards and Envelopes

ENVELOPE:

Mr. and Mrs. Simonsen

CARD:

Table No. 6

WEDDING
STATIONERY

INTRODUCTION AND CUSTOMS

"*Romance*" *is a word* we frequently associate with weddings. The romance of the wedding encourages us to practice customs that would, under other circumstances, seem outdated and unnecessary. Wedding customs were created to fill our ancestors' needs. Some were created out of necessity; others were ceremonial. As our needs have changed, we have refined these customs, but they continue to hold a place in today's wedding.

Brides and grooms exchange gold wedding rings, continuing a centuries old tradition. A ring is a never-ending circle symbolizing a husband and wife united forever. The ring is made of gold, a precious metal that never tarnishes. The first metal ring was used by Christians in 860 A.D. Centuries earlier, primitive man bound himself to his bride's waist with a cord of reeds, believing that the act would unite their spirits as one.

In days gone by, a man with the help of his loyal tribesmen invaded a neighboring town. While his tribesmen plundered and pillaged, he located the prettiest girl in town and carried her away. His tribesmen remained behind, to fend off her angry kinsmen and to keep them from pursuit.

After leaving town, the man and his bride hid from her kinsmen until their anger cooled. Their seclusion lasted thirty days or until the moon had waned. The Teutons tribe drank an elixir made from honey that they believed increased virility and fertility. And, so, the honeymoon was born.

The modern honeymoon is more likely a vacation on a Caribbean beach than an escape from family wrath. It is still, however, a period of seclusion from the rest of the world.

Although no longer needed to fend off angry kinsmen, the groom's friends are still at his side, serving as ushers and separating the "tribes" by seating the bride's family and the groom's family on opposite sides of the church. The best man assists the couple in leaving the wedding and going safely on their honeymoon. The woman is called the bride from the Anglo-Saxon word "bryd" meaning "one who is carried off."

Not all weddings were initiated by a kidnapping. Some were arranged. The couple's parents arranged the marriage, matching wealth, land, and titles instead of hearts. In many cases, the bride and groom were not even accorded the privilege of meeting each other until after the wedding. Indeed, the bride's presence was not always necessary. Similarly, young men arranged their own weddings with the prospective bride's father, negotiating the purchase price or the size of the dowry.

In deference to tradition, some men still ask a woman's father for her hand in marriage and the bride's father gives the bride away during the wedding ceremony. Today, the bride and groom may not see each other on their wedding day until they arrive at the altar, as that is considered bad luck.

The cutting of the wedding cake is one of the highlights of a modern wedding. The bride cuts the first piece, with the groom's hand over hers, and feeds her husband the first bite. He feeds her the second bite as they share their first "meal" together.

Wedding feasts and celebrations are as old as the ceremony itself. In Rome, the bride and groom shared a special cake, symbolizing their first meal together and a lifetime of prosperity. Greeks kneaded the dough for the wedding breads in public so that friends of the bride and groom would be able to toss coins into the dough as gifts for the wedding couple. The term "being in the dough" may have its origin in this custom.

Gifts are also bestowed upon the bride at a bridal shower. Legend has it that the first bridal shower was given when, once upon a time, a Dutch father refused to give his daughter her dowry. The young lady wanted to marry a miller who, although poor in the way of material possessions, was generous with what little he had. Whenever someone in the town needed help, the miller was the first to lend a hand.

The lady's father wanted her to marry a wealthy farmer whose livestock included more than a hundred pigs. She renounced her dowry to marry the miller.

When the recipients of the miller's generosity heard what the young lady had given up to marry the miller, they got together to see what they could do. Money was scarce among these peasants, so they gave simple, practical gifts to the miller and his bride. This showering of gifts produced a dowry finer than the one she renounced.

Moved by the generosity of the townspeople, her father added her dowry to their shower of good fortune. It is said that all lived happily ever after.

Weddings performed in England and colonial America required the public posting of the banns. The banns proclaimed the marriage intentions of the young people. They committed them to each other and to proscribed behavior. It is now no longer mandatory to post the banns. Instead, wedding invitations and announcements are sent to family and friends.

Our willingness to continue these and other wedding customs is testimony to the high esteem in which we hold the institution of marriage. When we marry, we continue a tradition and a way of life passed on to us through many generations. Our observance of this tradition marries us to the history and the values of our society.

Selecting Your Wedding Invitation

"First impressions count the most." You have probably heard that advice over and over again. It is sound advice and something to keep in mind when planning your wedding.

The first impressions of your wedding are formed long before your guests enter the church or step into the beautifully decorated reception hall. Their first impressions are formed weeks before the wedding when they receive your wedding invitations.

Your invitation should be a reflection of your ceremony and reception. It should be part of the total package and should set the tone for the wedding itself.

Wedding Papers

The best invitations are engraved on paper made from cotton. Paper has been made from cotton for nearly two thousand years. (Wood pulp has only been used since the late 1800s.) Paper made from 100-percent cotton fiber will give your wedding invitations a soft, rich feel. When you are at your stationer selecting your invitations, feel the papers. You will be able to tell the difference. Unlike wood-pulp papers, cotton-fiber papers do not decompose, so your invitations will last forever as keepsakes.

Your invitations can be engraved on either ecru (off-white) or white paper. Ecru is much more popular in the United States, but white is the color of choice in Europe. You should choose a relatively heavy paper. Better wedding papers are usually 40-pound papers. The weight of a paper is determined by the weight of a ream (500 sheets) of that paper cut to a standard size.

Wedding papers can be either plain or paneled. A paneled invitation has a blind embossed border. As a general rule, script lettering styles look better on an invitation without a panel. The extra space allows these calligraphic styles to spread across the page in all their glory. Print styles are usually tighter than script styles and generally look better inside a panel. The panel focuses your eye on the engraving.

Engraving and Thermography

Engraving from a copper plate offers you the most beautiful and distinctive look. Copperplate engraving dates back to the mid-seventeenth century when it gradually replaced calligraphy as the most commonly used method for making copies. Many of the engraving styles in use today can be traced back to old calligraphic styles. Engraving can be distinguished from other forms of printing by its sharp, distinctive lines, the subtle bruise on the front of the paper, and the indentation on the back caused by the pressure exerted by the copper plate. Many people actually look for these indications to see if invitations are engraved or not.

Thermography, also known as raised printing, is another method of printing that can be used for your invitations. It will give you a look similar to, but not quite as nice as, engraving. Thermography is, however, less expensive than engraving.

If cost is a factor, you may want to consider using thermography instead of engraving as opposed to using a lower quality paper. Many people who are not familiar with engraving and thermography, and who do not know what to look for, will be unable to tell the difference. Everybody, on the other hand, will be able to tell the difference between a 100-percent cotton-fiber paper and a wood-pulp paper even if they do not know why.

Folded and Unfolded Invitations

Most of us are accustomed to receiving wedding invitations with a fold along the left-hand side of the invitation. These invitations fit, without an additional fold, into a set of envelopes that are slightly larger than the invitations themselves. Today, the vast majority of invitations are sold this way.

However, that was not always the case. At one time, most formal social events were held in metropolitan areas. Houses and apartments in the cities had small mailboxes. To prevent the postman from forcing oversized envelopes into small mailboxes and, in effect, sloppily folding the invitations, engravers neatly folded the invitations in half (from top to bottom) and placed them in envelopes that were approximately half the size of the invitation.

Look at your parents' wedding invitations. They were probably folded in half. These traditional invitations are still available today, although their popularity has decreased.

Choosing a Lettering Style

There are literally hundreds of different lettering styles to choose from. Fortunately, most stationers limit your choices.

You should choose a lettering style that fits both the formality of the wedding and your personal taste. Your stationer can show you different styles, suggest the appropriate ones, and tell you which ones are most popular. Ultimately, you will decide according to your personal taste.

It is probably best for you to choose a classic or conservative lettering style for two reasons: (1) You, as well as your friends and family members, will undoubtedly save your wedding invitations as keepsakes. Classic lettering styles wear well. They will look as beautiful on your golden wedding anniversary as they do today. (2) Your wedding may well be the most formal event that you ever attend. Formal, classic invitations will fit the occasion.

Ink Color

Black ink is the correct choice for all formal invitations, and wedding invitations are no exception. Some heavy lettering styles, however, look better in a dark-gray ink (especially on white paper). When this is the case, you may use a dark-grey ink instead. Other colors, though, are too frivolous for formal wedding invitations.

Coat of Arms

A coat of arms may be used when the bride's family has one. It should be blind embossed at the top center of the invitation. If your family does not already own a coat of arms engraving die, you will need to order one. Most coat of arms dies are cut by hand and can take a couple of months to produce. You should keep this extra time in mind when considering a new coat of arms die.

Only a coat of arms die properly appears at the top of a wedding invitation. Doves, flowers, and monograms do not belong on a formal wedding invitation. Save them for something informal.

Phrasing

Wedding invitations are always phrased in the third person. The English spelling of "honour" and "favour" is usually used, although you may use "honor" and "favor" if you prefer.

Proper names should always be written out in full, including the middle name. Initials should never appear on a wedding invitation. If your fiance or father absolutely refuses to allow his middle name to appear on the invitation, drop it altogether and use just his first and last names. Your invitations will look much nicer without initials on them.

Abbreviations, except "Mr.," "Mrs.," "Dr.," and "Jr.," should not be used.

The formal presentation of "junior" on invitations is to spell it out. The j is lower case and preceded by a comma. Less formal, but also correct, is the use of the abbreviation, "Jr." The J is upper case and preceded by a comma.

The suffixes "II" and "III" are used on an invitation in the same way as "junior." They indicate that an older relative has the same name. The suffix "II" or "2nd" is used when a man is named after his grandfather or his uncle. The suffix "III" or "3rd" is used by the son of a man using "junior" or "II." These suffixes are usually dropped when the older relative dies. However, when the older relative is a well-known public figure, the suffixes are kept to distinguish the younger man from his well-known relative.

A comma usually precedes the suffixes "II" and "III," but some men prefer to omit it.

The words "Black tie" should not appear on formal invitations. The time of day (after six o'clock in the evening is considered formal) and the location determine the dress code. Although some people know when to dress formally, many do not. Therefore, you may wish to include "Black tie" on your invitations if you are not sure that all of your guests will know to dress formally. It is never proper, however, to use "Black tie preferred" as that can mean, although you would prefer that your guests showed up in black tie, it really does not matter to you how they dress. "Black tie" appears in the lower right-hand corner of the reception card since it is the reception that is formal.

Replies to invitations are requested by placing the reply request information in the lower left-hand corner of the invitations. When reception cards are sent with the invitations, the reply request appears on the reception cards, as guests reply to the reception, not to the ceremony.

"The favour of a reply is requested" can be used as a reply request and is especially favored in the South. "R.s.v.p." or "R.S.V.P." (either is correct) is short for the French "*Répondez s'il vous plaît.*" "Please reply" and "Please respond" are the English equivalents of "R.s.v.p." All of the above phrases can be used properly on invitations. The appearance of any of these on an invitation requires a reply from the recipient.

"Regrets only" can be used on invitations to a large cocktail party or buffet when an exact count on the number of guests is not necessary.

The address to which the replies should be sent appears beneath the reply request. An exception to this is when the event is being held at home and the address is given in the body of the invitation.

Replies are sent to the person (or persons in the case of Mr. and Mrs.) whose name appears first on the invitation, unless a different name is given in the reply request.

You may also send reply cards and envelopes. In the past, these have not strictly been considered proper, but they are now commonly used. If you use reply cards and envelopes, you should not show any reply request information on the invitations.

Composition of a Wedding Invitation

Mr. and Mrs. Paul James Travis

INVITATIONAL LINE

request the honour of your presence

REQUEST LINES

at the marriage of their daughter

Christina Lee

BRIDE'S NAME

to

JOINING CLAUSE

Mr. Allen Jay Fannin

GROOM'S NAME

Saturday, the sixth of June

DATE LINE

One thousand, nine hundred and ninety-five

YEAR LINE

at six o'clock

TIME LINE

Old First Presbyterian Church

LOCATION

125 Main Street

ADDRESS

Huntington, New York

CITY AND STATE

Invitational Line

The invitational line tells your guests who is extending the invitation. It gives them the names of the persons to whom they will send their replies. Wedding invitations are properly extended only by the parents of the bride. There are some exceptions to this rule, and they will be covered later on. When the parents are married to each other, their names appear as follows.

Mr. and Mrs. Paul James Travis

request the honour of your presence

at the marriage of their daughter

Christina Lee

etc.

DIVORCED MOTHER

Traditionally, a divorced woman who had not remarried used her maiden name and married name preceded by "Mrs." Today, a divorced woman who has not remarried may use her first name, maiden name, and married name preceded by "Mrs."

If she has remarried, she uses her husband's name preceded by "Mrs." The bride, in this case, uses her full name without her title since her surname is not the same as her mother's.

BRIDE'S MOTHER HAS NOT REMARRIED

Mrs. Simpson Travis
requests the honour of your presence
at the marriage of her daughter
Christina Lee
etc.

———————

Mrs. Laura Simpson Travis
requests the honour of your presence
at the marriage of her daughter
Christina Lee
etc.

BRIDE'S MOTHER HAS REMARRIED

Mrs. Glenn Lincoln Sanderson
requests the honour of your presence
at the marriage of her daughter
Christina Lee Travis
etc.

WIDOWED PARENTS

If one of the bride's parents is widowed, his or her name would appear alone on the first line of the invitation. A widow keeps her husband's name upon his death. If she remarries, she takes her new husband's name.

BRIDE'S FATHER

Mr. Paul James Travis

requests the honour of your presence

at the marriage of his daughter

Christina Lee

etc.

BRIDE'S MOTHER HAS NOT REMARRIED

Mrs. Paul James Travis

requests the honour of your presence

at the marriage of her daughter

Christina Lee

etc.

BRIDE'S MOTHER HAS REMARRIED

Mrs. Glenn Lincoln Sanderson

requests the pleasure of your company

at the marriage of her daughter

Christina Lee Travis

etc.

STEPPARENTS

Only the bride's mother and/or father issue the wedding invitations. Therefore, only their names properly appear on the invitations. Exceptions to this rule occur when the bride's stepparent helped raise her from a young age, and when the bride feels especially close to her stepparent.

BRIDE'S MOTHER AND STEPFATHER

Mr. and Mrs. Glenn Lincoln Sanderson

request the honour of your presence

at the marriage of Mrs. Sanderson's daughter

Christina Lee Travis

etc.

or

Mr. and Mrs. Glenn Lincoln Sanderson

request the honour of your presence

at the marriage of her daughter

Christina Lee Travis

etc.

BRIDE'S FATHER AND STEPMOTHER

Mr. and Mrs. Paul James Travis

request the honour of your presence

at the marriage of Mr. Travis' daughter

Christina Lee

etc.

or

Mr. and Mrs. Paul James Travis

request the honour of your presence

at the marriage of his daughter

Christina Lee

etc.

DIVORCED PARENTS

If the bride's parents are divorced and both names are to appear on the invitation, the name of the bride's mother appears on the first line and the name of the bride's father appears on the second line. The lines are not separated by "and."

DIVORCED PARENTS; BRIDE'S MOTHER HAS NOT REMARRIED

Mrs. Laura Simpson Travis

Mr. Paul James Travis

request the honour of your presence

at the marriage of their daughter

Christina Lee

etc.

DIVORCED PARENTS; BRIDE'S MOTHER HAS REMARRIED

Mrs. Glenn Lincoln Sanderson

Mr. Paul James Travis

request the honour of your presence

at the marriage of their daughter

Christina Lee

etc.

There are many emotions involved when dealing with divorced parents and their spouses. In most cases, everything is handled with love and understanding and few problems arise.

You might find yourself in a situation in which your parents cannot agree on whose name or names will appear on your invitations. You need to handle this balancing act with concern for everybody's feelings.

The most common problem occurs when the bride's father wants to make sure the guests know he paid for the wedding. Related to that, but not as common, is his desire to let the guests know he has remarried.

If you are in that situation, try to avoid using anybody's name except those of your parents on the invitation itself. If your parents do not want the invitation to "go by the book," you can use your mother's name alone at the top of the invitation to the ceremony and your father's name alone (or with that of his wife, if need be) at the top of the reception card. His name as host of the reception infers that he is paying for the reception. If your parents cannot agree to a compromise wording, you may issue the invitations with the groom. Your parents' names would not appear on these invitations.

The invitation and reception card would read:

Mrs. Laura Simpson Travis

requests the honour of your presence

at the marriage of her daughter

Christina Lee

etc.

Mr. Paul James Travis

requests the pleasure of your company

at the marriage reception

Saturday, the sixth of June

at seven o'clock

Huntington Bay Country Club

SEPARATED PARENTS

Parents who are separated but not divorced may issue the invitation as "Mr. and Mrs."

BRIDE'S MOTHER IS A DOCTOR

A married woman who is a medical doctor usually uses her social name on her daughter's wedding invitations. She and the bride's father are presented as "Mr. and Mrs."

The use of "Mr. and Dr." looks and sounds awkward. It also does not indicate that the bride's mother is a doctor since removing the "Mr. and" creates "Dr. Paul James Travis." To avoid this, some couples use their full names and titles (i.e., Mr. Paul James Travis and Dr. Laura Simpson Travis). It should be noted, however, that the two full names will probably not fit on a single line, and their appearance on separate lines may indicate to guests that the bride's parents are divorced. When both of the bride's parents are medical doctors, they may use "The Doctors."

The Doctors Travis

request the honour of your presence

at the marriage of their daughter

Christina Lee

etc.

PERSONS OTHER THAN THE BRIDE'S PARENTS

Another member of the bride's family or any close friend may issue the wedding invitations. This might occur when the bride's parents are not alive. If the invitations are issued by a relative, that relationship is shown on the third line. The bride's full name appears on the invitation. It is preceded by "Miss" when issued by friends but appears without "Miss" when issued by relatives.

BRIDE'S GRANDMOTHER

Mrs. Jeffrey Harold Travis
requests the honour of your presence
at the marriage of her granddaughter
Christina Lee Travis
etc.

FRIENDS OF THE BRIDE

Mr. and Mrs. John Kevin Murphey
request the honour of your presence
at the marriage of
Miss Christina Lee Travis
etc.

PARENTS OF THE GROOM

Although it is rarely done, the parents of the groom may issue the wedding invitations. The following format is used:

Mr. and Mrs. John Carlton Fannin

request the honour of your presence

at the marriage of

Miss Christina Lee Travis

to their son

Mr. Allen Jay Fannin

etc.

BRIDE AND GROOM

The bride and groom may wish to issue their own wedding invitations. This might be the case for the marriage of an older couple or for a second marriage. The most formal format would be written in the third person without the invitational line. The bride's name is preceded by "Miss."

The honour of your presence

is requested at the marriage of

Miss Christina Lee Travis

to

Mr. Allen Jay Fannin

etc.

or, less formally,

Miss Christina Lee Travis

and

Mr. Allen Jay Fannin

request the honour of your presence

at their marriage

etc.

SECOND MARRIAGES

When a bride is marrying for a second time, the couple usually extends the invitations themselves. The bride uses her present married name.

A divorced bride marrying for the second time uses either her maiden and married names preceded by "Mrs." or her first maiden and married names preceded by "Mrs." Subsequent marriages require the use of first, maiden, and most recent married names, preceded by "Mrs." Many brides prefer not to use "Mrs." and instead use their full names without a title. If you choose that course, you should omit the groom's title as well, so that the invitation retains its uniformity. A bride who legally uses her maiden name does not use a title on her wedding invitations.

A widowed bride uses her present married name. The bride's parents may issue invitations for a young bride who is widowed. The bride uses her full name without her title.

DIVORCED BRIDE

The honour of your presence
is requested at the marriage of
Mrs. Christina Travis Mackay
to
Mr. Allen Jay Fannin
etc.

or, less formally,

Christina Travis Mackay
and
Allen Jay Fannin
request the honour of your presence
at their marriage
etc.

DIVORCED BRIDE (NO TITLES)

The honour of your presence

is requested at the marriage of

Christina Travis Mackay

to

Allen Jay Fannin

etc.

or

Christina Travis Mackay

and

Allen Jay Fannin

request the honour of your presence

at their marriage

etc.

WIDOWED BRIDE

The honour of your presence

is requested at the marriage of

Mrs. Laurence Nelson Mackay

to

Mr. Allen Jay Fannin

etc.

YOUNG WIDOW

Mr. and Mrs. Paul James Travis
request the honour of your presence
at the marriage of their daughter
Christina Travis Mackay
etc.

Request Lines

The request lines invite your guests to your wedding. "Request the honour of your presence" is always used when the wedding ceremony is being held in a church, synagogue, or other house of worship. The use of "honour" (or "honor") shows deference and respect toward the house of worship. Invitations to a religious ceremony held at a place other than a house of worship do not properly use "request the honour of your presence."

The proper wording for a wedding ceremony held at home, at a club, or on a yacht is "request the pleasure of your company."

CHURCH, SYNAGOGUE, HOUSE OF WORSHIP

Mr. and Mrs. Paul James Travis
request the honour of your presence
at the marriage of their daughter
etc.

AT HOME, AT A CLUB, OR ON A YACHT

Mr. and Mrs. Paul James Travis

request the pleasure of your company

at the marriage of their daughter

etc.

Bride's Name

The bride's given names are shown on invitations issued by her parents. Her given names and surname appear on invitations when the surname of the issuer is different than that of the bride, for example, when the bride's mother is divorced and remarried. The bride's full name preceded by "Miss" is used when the bride and groom issue the invitations themselves.

When the bride is divorced, her full name (either maiden name and married name or first name, maiden name, and married name) preceded by "Mrs." appears on the invitation. The bride may wish to omit the "Mrs." In this case the groom's title is omitted as well. A divorced bride who legally uses her maiden name does not use a title on wedding invitations. "Ms." should never appear on wedding invitations.

A widow retains her husband's name, so she remains "Mrs. Laurence Nelson Mackay." Her full married name appears on the invitations unless she is a young widow, in which case her parents may issue the invitations. Her first name, maiden name, and married name appear on the invitations, without her title.

An annulment restores to a woman the right to use "Miss." An invitation for a second marriage, issued by parents, shows her complete maiden name, not just her given names. This distinguishes between a first and second marriage. When the bride and groom issue the invitations, she uses her full name preceded by "Miss."

ISSUED BY PARENTS

Mr. and Mrs. Paul James Travis
request the honour of your presence
at the marriage of their daughter
Christina Lee
etc.

ISSUED BY BRIDE'S MOTHER AND STEPFATHER

Mr. and Mrs. Glenn Lincoln Sanderson
request the honour of your presence
at the marriage of her daughter
Christina Lee Travis
etc.

ISSUED BY BRIDE AND GROOM

The honour of your presence
is requested at the marriage of
Miss Christina Lee Travis
to
Mr. Allen Jay Fannin
etc.

ISSUED BY DIVORCED BRIDE AND GROOM

The honour of your presence

is requested at the marriage of

Mrs. Christina Travis Mackay

to

Mr. Allen Jay Fannin

etc.

or

Christina Travis Mackay

and

Allen Jay Fannin

request the honour of your presence

at their marriage

etc.

ISSUED BY WIDOWED BRIDE AND GROOM

The honour of your presence

is requested at the marriage of

Mrs. Laurence Nelson Mackay

to

Mr. Allen Jay Fannin

etc.

ISSUED BY PARENTS OF A YOUNG WIDOW

Mr. and Mrs. Paul James Travis
request the honour of your presence
at the marriage of their daughter
Christina Travis Mackay
etc.

ISSUED BY PARENTS OF A WOMAN
WHOSE FIRST MARRIAGE WAS ANNULLED

Mr. and Mrs. Paul James Travis
request the honour of your presence
at the marriage of their daughter
Christina Lee Travis
etc.

BRIDE'S PROFESSIONAL TITLE

If a bride is a medical doctor, she uses "Doctor" or "Dr." on invitations issued by the bride and groom, or in any other instance in which the bride's title would normally appear. Her title should not appear on invitations issued by her parents. However, many brides are now including their titles on all invitations, feeling that it is unfair to have the groom's professional title appear when hers does not. After all, she worked as hard as he did to earn her degree.

ISSUED BY BRIDE'S PARENTS

Mr. and Mrs. Paul James Travis
request the honour of your presence
at the marriage of their daughter
Christina Lee
etc.

or

Mr. and Mrs. Paul James Travis
request the honour of your presence
at the marriage of their daughter
Dr. Christina Lee Travis
etc.

ISSUED BY BRIDE AND GROOM

The honour of your presence
is requested at the marriage of
Dr. Christina Lee Travis
to
Mr. Allen Jay Fannin
etc.

Joining Clauses

The word "to" is used to join the names of the bride and groom on invitations to the marriage ceremony. "And" is used on invitations to a marriage reception.

Groom's Name

The groom's full name, preceded by his title, should be used. While it is not proper to use initials on wedding invitations, some men dislike their middle names and would rather use their middle initial. Initials should never appear on wedding invitations. The invitations will look much better if the groom omits his middle name altogether, rather than using just his middle initial.

Date Line

The date line informs the recipient of the invitation of the date on which the wedding will take place. The day of the week and the date of the month are shown on this line. The day of the week may be preceded by "on," but it is equally proper to omit it.

Saturday, the sixth of June

or

on Saturday, the sixth of June

It is not necessary to use "morning," "afternoon," or "evening" on a wedding invitation. These terms are, however, occasionally used for weddings taking place at eight, nine, or ten o'clock. Usually, the time of day can be determined by reading the reception card. A breakfast is held before one o'clock; a reception is held at one o'clock or later.

Saturday evening, the sixth of June

or

on Saturday evening, the sixth of June

Year Line

The year need not appear on wedding invitations. Due to the immediacy of the event, the year is assumed. For instance, invitations are not mailed one year and four weeks before the wedding. Although not necessary, it is not improper to include the year. You may even wish to include it since many of your guests will be saving your invitations as keepsakes.

The year line is necessary on wedding announcements, as they announce an event that has already taken place. (Announcements are mailed after the wedding.)

The year may be presented two ways:

One thousand, nine hundred and ninety-five

or

Nineteen hundred and ninety-five

Time Line

It is said that it is good luck to be married on the half hour. The minute hand is moving up, and that is considered a good omen. If you get married on the hour, the minute hand is moving down, and your marriage will, so they say, be all down hill from there. The best of all possible worlds is to be married at noon when both hands are in the praying position.

The hour of the wedding always appears on one line, preceded by "at." No upper case letters are used. Twelve o'clock noon is expressed simply as "twelve o'clock." Your guests will assume that the wedding is taking place at noon and not at midnight.

The time line can also be used to express the time of the day. The terms "in the morning," "in the afternoon," and "in the evening" may follow the time. They would not be used, however, when the time of day is shown on the date line.

Examples:

at six o'clock

----

at twelve o'clock

----

at half after six o'clock

----

at quarter after six o'clock

----

at three quarters after six o'clock

----

at eight o'clock in the evening

Location

CHURCH NAME

The name of the church, temple, or club is given on the location line. The complete name of the location should be shown. If the word "Saint" part of the name, it should be spelled out. The correct name of a church known, for example, as Saint Michael's Church might actually be Church of Saint Michael. So, check with your church to confirm its correct name.

Old First Presbyterian Church

Church of Saint Michael

STREET ADDRESS

The street address is not necessary unless there are two churches with the same name in the same locality. It is not, however, incorrect to show the street address. The address may be given when the church is not widely known or when there are many out-of-town guests. The street address is never shown on the invitation when direction cards are used.

125 Main Street

Madison Avenue at Sixty-eighth Street

CITY AND STATE

The names of the city and state in which the wedding is being held always appear on the invitations. There are some exceptions to this rule. If your wedding is being held in New York City, you would use only "New York" or "New York City," since "New York, New York" seems redundant. Other usages include:

Huntington, New York

Washington, District of Columbia

in the City of Washington

Boston   *Massachusetts*

Ceremony and Reception at the Same Location

Reception cards are not necessary when the marriage ceremony and reception are held at the same place. A line reading, "and afterwards at the reception" may be added to the body of the invitation to indicate that the reception will follow the ceremony at the same location. If the reception is held at the church, the line may read, "and afterwards in the church parlours." This line appears as part of the body of the invitation beneath the city and state.

If reply cards and envelopes are not being used, the reply request information may be shown in the lower left-hand corner of the invitation. The first line reads, "R.s.v.p.," "R.S.V.P.," or "The favour of a reply is requested."

Mr. and Mrs. Paul James Travis

request the honour of your presence

at the marriage of their daughter

Christina Lee

to

Mr. Allen Jay Fannin

Saturday, the sixth of June

at six o'clock

Old First Presbyterian Church

Huntington, New York

and afterwards in the church parlours

Nuptial Mass

A Nuptial Mass is a Catholic Mass celebrating a wedding. The wording of an invitation to a Nuptial Mass varies slightly from that of a standard wedding invitation.

Mr. and Mrs. Paul James Travis

request the honour of your presence

at the Nuptial Mass at which their daughter

Christina Lee

and

Mr. Allen Jay Fannin

will be united in the Sacrament of Holy Matrimony

Saturday, the sixth of June

at ten o'clock

Saint Patrick's Cathedral

New York

Traditional Jewish Invitations

In contrast to the Christian custom, where the bride's family gives the bride away, the Jewish custom celebrates the uniting of two families. Therefore, the names of both sets of parents appear on the invitation. The names of the groom's parents appear at the top of the invitation beneath the names of the bride's parents. When this is done, the names of the bride and groom are joined by "and," not by "to."

Another wording that is also proper shows the names of the groom's parents beneath the groom's name. A line reading, "son of" separates the names.

Mr. and Mrs. Herman Benjamin Dreksler

Dr. and Mrs. Richard Samuel Abrams

request the honour of your presence

at the marriage of

Sarah Lynn Dreksler

and

Hillel Alan Abrams

Sunday, the tenth of May

at eight o'clock

Temple Sholom

Chicago, Illinois

or

Mr. and Mrs. Herman Benjamin Dreksler

request the honour of your presence

at the marriage of their daughter

Sarah Lynn

to

Dr. Hillel Alan Abrams

son of

Dr. and Mrs. Richard Samuel Abrams

Sunday, the tenth of May

at eight o'clock

Temple Sholom

Chicago, Illinois

Hispanic Weddings

Invitations to an Hispanic wedding are issued by both sets of parents. The copy is engraved on the inside of the invitations. An invitation from the bride's family appears on the left inside page, while an invitation from the groom's family appears on the right inside page. The invitation copy from both invitations may join when common information, such as the date, time, and place, is given. The invitations may also be engraved on the front page with the names of both sets of parents appearing at the top.

José Hernandez Caratini

Carmen María de Hernandez

request the honour of your presence

at the marriage of their daughter

Linda

to

Roberto Martinez

Juan Martinez Garza

Consuela Elena de Martinez

request the honour of your presence

at the marriage of

Linda Hernandez

to their son

Roberto

Saturday, the tenth of July

One thousand, nine hundred and ninety-five

at two o'clock

Santa Iglesia Cathedral

San Juan, Puerto Rico

José Hernandez Caratini
Carmen Maria de Hernandez
y
Juan Martinez Garza
Consuela Elena de Martinez
tienen el honor de invitarle
al matrimonio de sus hijos
Linda
y
Roberto
el sabado diez de Julio
de mil novecientos noventa y cinco
a las dos de la tarde
Santa Iglesia Catedral
San Juan de Puerto Rico

Double Wedding Ceremony

The elder sister's name appears first on invitations for a double wedding ceremony for sisters. When a double wedding is performed for brides who are not sisters, it is best to send two separate invitations.

Mr. and Mrs. Paul James Travis

request the honour of your presence

at the marriage of their daughters

Christina Lee

to

Mr. Allen Jay Fannin

and

Stephanie Jane

to

Mr. Robert Stuart Martin

Saturday, the sixth of June

at six o'clock

Old First Presbyterian Church

Huntington, New York

Guest's Name Written In

The guest's name is written in, usually in calligraphy on the most formal invitations. Personalizing the invitations in this way honors the guest. A personalized invitation may also be used in lieu of an admission card.

Mr. and Mrs. Paul James Travis

request the honour of the presence of

Mr. and Mrs. Mark McCay
at the marriage of their daughter

Christina Lee

etc.

Invitation to a Wedding at Home

When your wedding is being held at the home of the person(s) extending the invitation (your parents' home, for example), their address appears on the location line. "The favour of a reply is requested" or "R.s.v.p." appear alone in the lower left-hand corner (or not at all if reply cards and envelopes are being used). There is no need to put the reply address beneath "R.s.v.p." since the address is already given in the body of the invitation. The wedding is not being held in a house of worship, so "request the pleasure of your company" should be used.

Mr. and Mrs. Paul James Travis

request the pleasure of your company

at the marriage of their daughter

Christina Lee

to

Mr. Allen Jay Fannin

Saturday, the sixth of June

at six o'clock

307 West Shore Road

Huntington, New York

Invitation to a Wedding at the Residence of . . .

A wedding held at the home of someone other than the person(s) who issued the invitations requires a line reading "at the residence of," followed by a line with the names of the people at whose home the wedding is being held. Replies are always sent to the person(s) whose name(s) appears first on the invitations unless a different name is given with the reply information. The request line reads "request the pleasure of your company," since the wedding is not being held in a house of worship.

Mr. and Mrs. Paul James Travis

request the pleasure of your company

at the marriage of their daughter

Christina Lee

to

Mr. Allen Jay Fannin

Saturday, the sixth of June

at six o'clock

at the residence of

Mr. and Mrs. Robert Anthony Dignon

106 Cove Road

Huntington, New York

Invitation to a Wedding at a Club

When the marriage ceremony and reception are being celebrated at a club or hotel, a line reading "and afterwards at the reception" or "and afterward at the reception" may be added to the body of the invitation beneath the city and state.

If reply cards and envelopes are not being used, the reply request information may appear in the lower left-hand corner of the invitation.

Since the ceremony is not being held in a house of worship, the request line reads "request the pleasure of your company."

Mr. and Mrs. Paul James Travis

request the pleasure of your company

at the marriage of their daughter

Christina Lee

to

Mr. Allen Jay Fannin

Saturday, the sixth of June

at six o'clock

Huntington Bay Country Club

Huntington, New York

and afterwards at the reception

Invitation to a Marriage Reception

Many brides, in particular those marrying for a second time, prefer a small, private ceremony attended by close friends and family members. Their private ceremony may be followed by a much larger reception.

When more people are invited to the reception than to the ceremony, marriage reception invitations are sent. Ceremony cards are enclosed with the invitations being sent to those guests who are also invited to the ceremony. The ceremony cards may be engraved or, when the ceremony is intimate, handwritten.

Ceremony cards should be formally worded. Although they are the same size as reception cards, they should be worded as formally as a full invitation.

The word "wedding" may be substituted for "marriage" when wording the invitations or ceremony cards. The word "and" replaces "to" on reception invitations.

Mr. and Mrs. Paul James Travis

request the pleasure of your company

at the marriage reception of their daughter

Christina Lee

and

Mr. Allen Jay Fannin

Saturday, the sixth of June

at seven o'clock

Huntington Bay Country Club

Huntington, New York

CEREMONY CARD

Mr. and Mrs. Paul James Travis
request the honour of your presence
at the marriage ceremony
Saturday, the sixth of June
at six o'clock
Old First Presbyterian Church

Late Reception

Receptions held after the wedding date are not properly referred to as marriage receptions. They are parties given in honor of the married couple. They may be given for any reason, but are usually given when the wedding is held in a town other than the one in which

Mr. and Mrs. John Carlton Fannin
request the pleasure of your company
at a party in honour of
Mr. and Mrs. Allen Jay Fannin
Saturday, the twenty-second of August
at eight o'clock
3608 Clubhouse Lane
Boca Raton, Florida

the bride and groom's parents and friends reside. Late receptions are also frequently held after a second marriage. Invitations sent for a late reception are never sent with wedding announcements. The reception is a separate event and requires a separate mailing.

Handwritten Invitations

The most personal wedding invitation is handwritten. If you are having a small wedding, your invitations should be written by hand, and may or may not follow the standard wedding format. They can be personal letters to each of your guests telling them that you are getting married and what the specifics are. The formality of the wording of your invitations depends on your closeness to the guest. The wording of the invitations need not be identical.

Handwritten invitations are written in black or dark-blue ink on ecru or white letter sheets. Letter sheets are formal sheets of paper with a fold along the left-hand side (like standard wedding invitations). They fold in half again from top to bottom and are mailed in a single envelope that is slightly larger than half the size of the letter sheet. There should be no monogram, coat of arms, or other embellishment at the top of the sheet.

Military Weddings

Wedding invitations involving members of the armed services follow the same etiquette as civilian weddings, with the exception of the use of military titles and service designations. Army, Air Force, and Marine officers with the rank of captain and higher and Navy officers with the rank of commander and higher use their military titles before their names. Their service designation appears on a line beneath their names. An exception is an invitation issued by an officer and his wife, in which case the service-designation line does not appear.

Junior officers do not use their titles before their names. Their titles appear on the following line, before their service designation.

Noncommissioned officers show only their service designations. Their rank does not appear on the invitations.

BRIDE'S FATHER IS AN OFFICER

When the bride's father is an officer and issues the wedding invitations with his wife, his military title precedes his name. There is no line denoting his branch of service. If he is retired, his retired status is not noted.

If the bride's father issues the invitations himself, his title precedes his name. The following line shows his service designation and his retired status, if appropriate.

Admiral and Mrs. Paul James Travis

request the honour of your presence

at the marriage of their daughter

Christina Lee

etc.

Admiral Paul James Travis

United States Navy, Retired

requests the honour of your presence

at the marriage of his daughter

Christina Lee

etc.

BRIDE'S MOTHER IS AN OFFICER

The bride's mother may use her military title on wedding invitations when she issues the invitations herself or when she is divorced and issues them jointly with the bride's father.

If she is married to the bride's father, she usually uses her social title "Mrs." As noted previously, it is not improper to use both parents' full names and titles. However, their appearance on separate lines may indicate to guests that they are divorced.

Captain Laura Simpson Travis

United States Navy, Retired

requests the honour of your presence

at the marriage of her daughter

Christina Lee

etc.

Mr. and Mrs. Paul James Travis

request the honour of your presence

at the marriage of their daughter

Christina Lee

etc.

BRIDE'S PARENTS ARE DIVORCED

The bride's parents may issue the wedding invitations jointly when they are divorced. The name of the bride's mother appears on the first line followed by the name of the bride's father.

Mrs. Laura Simpson Travis

Admiral Paul James Travis

United States Navy, Retired

request the honour of your presence

at the marriage of their daughter

Christina Lee

etc.

or

Captain Laura Simpson Travis

United States Navy, Retired

and

Admiral Paul James Travis

United States Navy, Retired

request the honour of your presence

at the marriage of their daughter

Christina Lee

etc.

BRIDE IS IN THE SERVICE

When the bride is an officer in the armed services, she uses her title in the same manner as would other members of the armed services.

Admiral and Mrs. Paul James Travis

request the honour of your presence

at the marriage of their daughter

Commander Christina Lee Travis

United States Navy

etc.

or

116

Admiral and Mrs. Paul James Travis

request the honour of your presence

at the marriage of their daughter

Christina Lee Travis

Ensign, United States Navy

etc.

GROOM IS IN THE SERVICE

The groom uses his title and service designation in the same manner as would other members of the armed services.

Admiral and Mrs. Paul James Travis

request the honour of your presence

at the marriage of their daughter

Commander Christina Lee Travis

United States Navy

to

Captain Allen Jay Fannin

United States Navy

etc.

Postponement of a Wedding

A wedding may need to be postponed due to illness or an unexpected death in the family. If time permits, engraved or printed announcements can be mailed to the invited guests. Telephone, telegram, or mailgram notices may be sent when there is insufficient time to send a more formal announcement.

Mr. and Mrs. Paul James Travis

announce that the marriage of their daughter

Christina Lee

to

Mr. Allen Jay Fannin

has been postponed to

Saturday, the sixteenth of August

at six o'clock

Old First Presbyterian Church

Huntington, New York

Invitation Recalled

When a wedding is to be postponed but no new date has been set, the invitation must be recalled. If time constraints do not allow for formal announcements, the invitations may be recalled by telephone, telegram, or mailgram. New invitations are sent once a new date has been set.

Mr. and Mrs. Paul James Travis

regret that the illness of their daughter

Christina Lee

obliges them to recall their invitations

to her marriage to

Mr. Allen Jay Fannin

on Saturday, the sixth of June

NEW INVITATION FOLLOWING RECALL

Mr. and Mrs. Paul James Travis

announce that the wedding of their daughter

Christina Lee

to

Mr. Allen Jay Fannin

which was postponed, will now take place

on Saturday, the sixteenth of August

at six o'clock

Old First Presbyterian Church

Huntington, New York

Cancellation of a Wedding Invitation

If a wedding is to be canceled, an engraved or printed announcement may be sent. Notice may be given by telephone, telegram, or mailgram when time does not permit a formal announcement.

Mr. and Mrs. Paul James Travis

are obliged to recall their invitations

to the marriage of their daughter

Christina Lee

to

Mr. Allen Jay Fannin

as the marriage will not take place

Wedding Announcements

Wedding announcements are sent to family members, friends, and business associates who were not invited to the wedding ceremony. They merely announce the event—they do not invite, nor do they require the recipient to send a gift.

Announcements are sent after the wedding takes place, never before. It is preferable to mail them the day after the wedding, but they may properly be sent up to one year after the wedding.

The announcements should be engraved or imprinted in black ink on an ecru or white letter sheet like the invitations. They are mailed in double envelopes. Although the wording of wedding announcements differs from that of invitations, the etiquette is the same.

When the wedding ceremony is held at a church, synagogue, or other house of worship, the name of the house of worship is included on the announcement. The location is generally not included in the announcement when the wedding ceremony is not held in a house of worship.

Wedding announcements announce a past event, so it is necessary to show the year. The year may be shown as:

One thousand, nine hundred and ninety-five

or

Nineteen hundred and ninety-five

Invitations to social events should not be mailed with announcements. If you are having a late reception, you should send the invitations separately.

Issued by Parents—Church Ceremony

Mr. and Mrs. Paul James Travis

have the honour of announcing

the marriage of their daughter

Christina Lee

to

Mr. Allen Jay Fannin

Saturday, the sixth of June

One thousand, nine hundred and ninety-five

Old First Presbyterian Church

Huntington, New York

Issued by Parents—at Home or at a Club

Mr. and Mrs. Paul James Travis

have the honour of announcing

the marriage of their daughter

Christina Lee

to

Mr. Allen Jay Fannin

Saturday, the sixth of June

Nineteen hundred and ninety-five

Huntington, New York

Issued by Bride and Groom—Church Ceremony

Miss Christina Lee Travis

and

Mr. Allen Jay Fannin

announce their marriage

Saturday, the sixth of June

One thousand, nine hundred and ninety-five

Old First Presbyterian Church

Huntington, New York

or, less formally

Christina Lee Travis

and

Allen Jay Fannin

announce their marriage

Saturday, the sixth of June

One thousand, nine hundred and ninety-five

Old First Presbyterian Church

Huntington, New York

Enclosure Cards

Reception Cards

Reception cards invite your guests to the wedding reception. They are sent with the invitation when the ceremony and the reception are being held at different locations. Reception cards serve as invitations to a separate event, so they should always be sent when your reception is not being held immediately following the ceremony at the same location. It is not proper to put reception information on the invitation to the ceremony when the reception is being held at a different location. When the ceremony and the reception are being held at the same location, you should not use reception cards.

OCCASION LINE

The occasion line tells your guests what the occasion will be. A breakfast takes place before one o'clock. A reception takes place at one o'clock or later. Although not strictly proper, some brides use "Dinner Reception" so that their guests will know not to make other arrangements for dinner.

TIME LINE

The second line is the time line. It usually reads "immediately following the ceremony." Some people argue that this wording gives the impression the reception "immediately" follows the ceremony and will create a stampede from the church to the reception hall, as guests rush to get to the reception on time. They would rather have the time line read "following the ceremony," although that may seem rather vague and could mean an hour later or several weeks later.

You should use "immediately following the ceremony," as it is generally accepted to mean approximately the amount of time it takes to get from the ceremony to the reception. If your reception starts two hours or more after the ceremony, you should put the time ("at eight o'clock") instead of "immediately following the ceremony."

LOCATION LINE

The third line indicates the place where the reception will be held. If the ceremony and reception are being held in different towns, a fourth line showing the city and state should be added.

CORNER LINES

The reply request and the address appear on the lower left-hand corner of the reception card. "R.s.v.p." is followed by the address of the person(s) extending the invitation. If someone other than the person(s) issuing the invitations are to receive the replies, that person's name should appear beneath "R.s.v.p." It is equally correct to use either "R.s.v.p." or "The favour of a reply is requested."

When reply cards and envelopes are being sent with the invitation, the corner lines on the reception card should read "R.s.v.p." or "The favour of a reply is requested." They may also be omitted entirely. It is not necessary to show the address, as that would appear on the reply envelope.

RECEPTION HELD AT A CLUB

Reception

immediately following the ceremony

Huntington Bay Country Club

R.s.v.p.
307 West Shore Road
Huntington, New York 11743

RECEPTION HELD AT HOME

Reception

immediately following the ceremony

307 West Shore Road

The favour of a reply is requested

RECEPTION HELD AT THE HOME OF
ANOTHER PERSON

Reception
at seven o'clock
at the residence of
Mr. and Mrs. Robert Anthony Dignan
106 Cove Road

R.s.v.p.
307 West Shore Road
Huntington, New York 11743

RECEPTION HELD ON A YACHT

Reception

immediately following the ceremony

aboard the Sea Treasure

Huntington Yacht Club

R. s. v. p.
307 West Shore Road
Huntington, New York 11743

The Sea Treasure
sails promptly at eight o'clock

RECEPTION HOSTED BY FATHER OF BRIDE

Mr. Paul James Travis

requests the pleasure of your company

at the marriage reception

immediately following the ceremony

Huntington Bay Country Club

Huntington

The favour of a reply is requested
800 Fifth Avenue
New York, New York 10021

129

At Home Cards

The address of the newly married couple is presented on the at home card. The etiquette for at home cards sent with invitations and announcements differs.

Wedding announcements are sent after the wedding has taken place, so the bride and groom use their new married names, their address, and the date after which they will be residing at that address. The at home card is usually the first official presentation of the newlyweds as Mr. and Mrs.

At home cards sent with wedding invitations cannot show the couple's married names since they are not married when the invitations are sent out. They cannot use Mr. and Mrs., so their names are not shown.

A bride who intends to keep her maiden name can use an at home card to subtly inform the recipients of this. The at home cards show her maiden name, her husband's name (both without titles), their address, and the date after which they will be residing at that address. These work especially well when sent with announcements, since the bride can be presented as Mrs. at the time the announcements are sent.

SENT WITH ANNOUNCEMENTS

Mr. and Mrs. Allen Jay Fannin

after the first of July

233 East 73rd Street
New York, New York 10021

SENT WITH INVITATIONS

At home

after the first of July

233 East 73rd Street

New York, New York 10021

BRIDE RETAINS HER MAIDEN NAME

Christina Lee Travis

Allen Jay Fannin

after the first of July

233 East 73rd Street

New York, New York 10021

Reply Cards and Envelopes

Wedding invitations are properly responded to with a handwritten note, written on a plain, folded letter sheet. Although a large majority of wedding invitations are sold with reply cards, they are still considered impersonal and improper. They are, however, becoming more and more acceptable.

People are raised more informally than they were in the past. Fewer people know how to respond properly to wedding invitations. This situation will surely continue indefinitely, as we all become more accustomed to receiving reply cards.

Reply cards should provide a space for the guest's name and a space for the response. Most reply cards request a reply before a specified date (usually two weeks before the wedding).

A space on the reply card reading "number of guests" should not appear, as that may give the impression that a guest is welcome to invite others to the wedding. Likewise, spaces requesting a menu choice (fish, chicken, or beef) should never appear.

Some brides prefer a handwritten response but do not trust their guests to reply on their own stationery. Their solution is to send a reply card with just "The favour of a reply is requested" in the lower left-hand corner.

Reply envelopes have the name and address of the person to whom the response is being sent engraved on the face of the envelope. The name and address are usually staggered but may be centered instead. A postage stamp is always affixed to the reply envelope.

REPLY CARDS

The favour of a reply

is requested before the twentieth of May

M _____

will _____ attend

M _____

will _____ attend

The favour of a reply
is requested before the twentieth of May

The favour of a reply is requested

REPLY ENVELOPE

Staggered Copy:

Mr. and Mrs. Paul James Travis
307 West Shore Road
Huntington, New York 11743

Centered Copy:

Mr. and Mrs. Paul James Travis
307 West Shore Road
Huntington, New York 11743

Ceremony Cards

Ceremony cards are enclosed with invitations to a marriage reception. When a large reception and a small ceremony are planned, an invitation to the reception, accompanied by a ceremony card, is mailed. The ceremony card is only sent with the invitations addressed to those guests who are also invited to the ceremony.

Since the ceremony is a formal service, a formal wording is appropriate. There is no need to include the names of the bride and groom, as that information is given on the reception invitation. The terms "marriage ceremony" and "wedding ceremony" are used interchangeably.

Mr. and Mrs. Paul James Travis
request the honour of your presence
at the marriage ceremony
Saturday, the sixth of June
at six o'clock
Old First Presbyterian Church

A less formal wording is:

Ceremony
at six o'clock
Old First Presbyterian Church

Direction Cards

Direction cards are used when a ceremony or reception is held at a location that is not widely known. Concise and explicit directions are given on the card. Direction cards that are engraved to match your invitations compliment the invitations. Directions cards furnished by churches and banquet halls and xeroxed copies do not.

FROM NEW YORK CITY:

LONG ISLAND EXPRESSWAY EAST TO EXIT 49N (ROUTE 110). FOLLOW ROUTE 110 FOR 7.5 MILES TO MAIN STREET. MAKE A RIGHT. DRIVE 1 MILE. CHURCH IS ON THE LEFT AT TOP OF HILL.

FROM EASTERN LONG ISLAND:

LONG ISLAND EXPRESSWAY WEST TO EXIT 49N (ROUTE 110). FOLLOW DIRECTIONS ABOVE.

Accommodation Cards

Accommodation cards are sent to out-of-town guests who need to make hotel arrangements. The card lists the names and phone numbers of convenient hotels. If the host has reserved and paid for a room for a guest, this would be stated on the card along with the hotel's address and phone number.

Accommodations

Anchorage Inn
(516) 555-1212

Huntington Hilton
(516) 555-1212

A room for you has been reserved at:
Anchorage Inn
1550 Mill Dam Road
Huntington, New York
(516) 555-1212

Transportation Cards

When transportation has been arranged for the guests, transportation cards should be enclosed with the invitations. This card is often sent to young people invited to a Bar/Bat Mitzvah reception, indicating that their transportation home will be provided.

Transportation will be provided
from the ceremony to the reception

or

Transportation home after the reception
will be provided

Pew Cards

Honored guests may be seated in a special section at the front of the church. To assist the ushers in seating these guests, pew cards are presented. Pew cards are sent with the invitation. The pew number is written in by hand, usually in calligraphy.

Please present this card at
Old First Presbyterian Church
Saturday, the sixth of June

Pew number 5

Within the Ribbon Cards

Cards reading "Within the Ribbon" inform the ushers that guests should be seated in a special section identified with a ribbon or cord.

Admission Cards

Admission cards are used when a celebrity or dignitary wishes to admit only invited guests to their wedding. The cards serve as tickets and must be presented by the guest. Formal invitations on which the guest's name is handwritten may also be used as admission cards.

Please present this card at
Old First Presbyterian Church
Saturday, the sixth of June

or

Mrs. Edward Cummings
will please present this card at
Old First Presbyterian Church
Saturday, the sixth of June

Assembling the Invitation

Before the advent of the post office, invitations were delivered by footmen. Due to the nature of his occupation, the footman's hands were dirty and soiled. Any correspondence that he delivered became soiled as well. To avoid the embarrassment of a guest receiving an invitation in a soiled envelope, invitations were delivered in two envelopes. The soiled outer envelope would be discarded, and the invitation would be presented in the clean inner envelope. The inner envelope showed just the names of those receiving the invitation. There was no address on it, as the invitation was already at its destination. The custom of mailing a wedding invitation in double envelopes endures to this day.

The invitation and enclosure cards are placed in the inner envelope in size order. The invitation is first. The largest enclosure is placed, faceup, on top (not inside) of the invitation. The next largest is then placed on top, and so on. The usual order is invitation, reception card, reply envelope (facedown), and reply card. All enclosures are inserted faceup except the reply envelope. The reply envelope is inserted facedown with the reply card (faceup), under its flap.

All of the enclosures are placed in the inner envelope with the fold of the invitation at the bottom of the envelope. Upon its removal, a right-handed person should be able to read the invitation.

The formal traditional invitations fold horizontally across the middle and fit into envelopes approximately half their size. In that case, the enclosures are placed in size order inside the invitation's first fold. The invitation is placed in the inner envelope folded end first so that, when it is removed, a right-handed person would be able to read it.

The inner envelope should face toward the back of the outer envelope, so that the names written on it appear right-side-up when it is removed from the envelope.

1. A single-fold invitation inserted into an envelope

2. Inserting a single-fold invitation with an enclosure card

3. A twice-fold invitation inserted into an envelope

4. Inserting a twice-folded invitation with an enclosure card

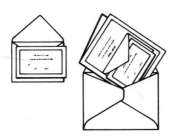

5. Enclosing a reply card and envelope

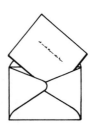

6. Placing an inner envelope into an outer envelope

Tissues

Invitations were once engraved with oil-based inks. These inks were very slow to dry, so tissue was inserted between the invitations to prevent smudging. Etiquette once called for removing the tissue, since it was just packing material and served no purpose.

However, many people failed to remove the tissue, and, through usage, tissued wedding invitations became acceptable and eventually were considered elegant. Today, most inks are water-based and dry rapidly. Tissuing is not necessary anymore, but it has become so associated with elegance and good taste that it is now considered proper.

Addressing the Wedding Envelopes

Calligraphy is the art of beautiful handwriting. Before the invention of the printing press, only a few members of the nobility and the clergy were able to read and write. Bibles, books, and official documents were penned by hand by scribes. These scribes developed a style of ornate handwriting known as calligraphy. The printing press gradually replaced the scribe, but the art of calligraphy endures to this day.

The rules of etiquette apply as much to addressing the envelope as they do to wording the invitation. Wedding invitations are mailed in two envelopes. They may be addressed in your own handwriting in black or dark-blue ink, or they may be addressed by a calligrapher.

The outer envelope is the mailing envelope. The recipient's name and address appear on the face of the envelope. The name and address may be staggered or centered. The sender's return address traditionally appears on the back flap of the envelope, although the post office prefers the return address to appear on the front of the envelope. No names appear with the return address, so if you live in an apartment building you must include your apartment number. The return address should be blind embossed, although some people prefer to engrave it in black ink.

Only the recipient's surname, preceded by a title, appears on the inner envelope.

Abbreviations should not appear on the envelopes except in the case of a title. "Dr.," "Mr.," "Mrs.," "Ms.," or "Jr." are acceptable. Although "Ms." is too informal to appear on wedding invitations, it may be used on the wedding envelopes. The rules of etiquette are the same for invitations and envelopes with the exception of the use of "Ms."

The terms "and guest" and "and escort" (as in "Miss Strickland and escort" or "Mr. Keegan and guest") should not be used on wedding envelopes. If you would like one of your guests to bring a friend, ask for the friend's name and address and send him or her a separate invitation. It is much nicer and much more personal to send a separate invitation than to add "and escort" to another person's invitation.

Likewise, "and family" should not appear on the envelopes. It is too impersonal and too ambiguous. Invitations that are extended to several members of the family should be addressed to the parents. The names of the children who are invited are written on the inner envelope beneath their parents' names. Older children living at home with their parents should receive separate invitations.

Back Flap of Outer Envelope

307 WEST SHORE ROAD
HUNTINGTON, NEW YORK 11743

or

APARTMENT 12C
233 EAST 73RD STREET
NEW YORK, NEW YORK 10021

Married Couple

OUTER ENVELOPE

Mr. and Mrs. William Edward Lipton
458 Habersham Road, N.W.
Atlanta, Georgia 30305

INNER ENVELOPE

Mr. and Mrs. Lipton

Married Couple with Children Under
Eighteen Living at Home

OUTER ENVELOPE

Mr. and Mrs. William Edward Lipton
458 Habersham Road, N.W.
Atlanta, Georgia 30305

INNER ENVELOPE

Mr. and Mrs. Lipton
Beth and Louise

Children Over Eighteen Living at Home

OUTER ENVELOPE

The Misses (or Messrs.) Lipton
458 Habersham Road, N.W.
Atlanta, Georgia 30305

INNER ENVELOPE

The Misses (or Messrs.) Lipton

Married Couple—Woman Kept Maiden Name

OUTER ENVELOPE

Ms. Elaine Lorinda Atkins
Mr. William Edward Lipton
458 Habersham Road, N.W.
Atlanta, Georgia 30305

INNER ENVELOPE

Ms. Atkins
Mr. Lipton

Married Couple—Both Are Doctors

OUTER ENVELOPE

The Doctors Lipton
458 Habersham Road, N.W.
Atlanta, Georgia 30305

INNER ENVELOPE

The Doctors Lipton

Married Couple—Woman Is a Doctor

OUTER ENVELOPE

Dr. Elaine Lorinda Atkins
Mr. William Edward Lipton
458 Habersham Road, N.W.
Atlanta, Georgia 30305

INNER ENVELOPE

Dr. Atkins
Mr. Lipton

Divorced Woman

OUTER ENVELOPE

Mrs. (Ms.) Elaine Atkins Lipton
458 Habersham Road, N.W.
Atlanta, Georgia 30305

INNER ENVELOPE

Mrs. (Ms.) Lipton

Widow

OUTER ENVELOPE

Mrs. William Edward Lipton
458 Habersham Road
Atlanta, Georgia 30305

INNER ENVELOPE

Mrs. Lipton

Man and Woman Living Together

OUTER ENVELOPE

Ms. Elaine Lorinda Atkins
Mr. William Edward Lipton
458 Habersham Road, N.W.
Atlanta, Georgia 30305

INNER ENVELOPE

Ms. Atkins
Mr. Lipton

Single Man

OUTER ENVELOPE

Mr. James Keith Mathews
50 Devonshire Lane
Kenilworth, Illinois 60045

INNER ENVELOPE

Mr. Mathews

Single Woman

OUTER ENVELOPE

Miss (Ms.) Ashley Crane Read
3738 Diamond Head Road
Honolulu, Hawaii 96815

INNER ENVELOPE

Miss (Ms.) Read

Mailing the Invitations

Wedding invitations should be mailed four to six weeks prior to the wedding. They should be ordered early enough to allow both the engraver and the calligrapher sufficient time to process the invitations and envelopes. As it is best to allow the engraver four to six weeks and the calligrapher an additional two weeks, invitations should be ordered at least three months prior to the wedding. The invitations should be weighed to determine the correct postage. The added weight of the enclosure cards may require additional postage.

Invitations should be mailed to all those the bride and groom wish to invite, including all relatives of the bride and groom, close friends and business associates of their families, the parents of the groom, members of the wedding party and their spouses, and the minister and his or her spouse. Enough invitations should be ordered to cover all those on the mailing list plus any surprises. Generally, an additional twenty-five to fifty will suffice. It is also advisable to order additional envelopes to cover any mistakes made in addressing.

Replying to Wedding Invitations

Replies to wedding invitations should be made promptly. The bride will be very busy attending to all the details of her wedding. You can assist her by replying as quickly as possible.

Wedding invitations are issued in the third person. Therefore, replies are made in the third person. The reply is made on a plain ecru or white letter sheet. It is written on the front, never on the inside, of the letter sheet in black or dark-blue ink. If a plain letter sheet is unavailable, a reply may be made on a sheet of conservative engraved stationery.

Accept

> Mr. and Mrs. Eric Randall Carr
> accept with pleasure
> the kind invitation of
> Mr. and Mrs. Travis
> for Saturday, the sixth of June
> at six o'clock

Regret

> Mr. and Mrs. Eric Randall Carr
> regret that they are unable to accept
> the kind invitation of
> Mr. and Mrs. Travis
> for Saturday, the sixth of June

Filling In Reply Cards

Reply cards are sent with invitations for the recipient's convenience. They should be returned promptly. Your name, preceded by your title (that is what the "M" is for), appears on the line. If you will be attending you leave the space blank. If you will not be attending you write in "not."

ACCEPT

M r. and Mrs. Cecil Bogart

will ———— attend

*A reply is requested
before the twentieth of May*

REGRET

M r. and Mrs. Peter Wilson

will __not__ attend

*A reply is requested
before the twentieth of May*

Rehearsal Dinner Invitations

The groom's parents usually issue the invitations to the rehearsal dinner. The dinner is given in honor of the bride and groom.

Mr. and Mrs. John Carlton Fanning

request the pleasure of your company

at a rehearsal dinner

in honour of

Miss Christina Lee Travis

and

Mr. Allen Jay Fanning

Friday, the fifth of June

at eight o'clock

Le Cote Basque

New York

Engagement Announcements

There is no formal etiquette for engagement announcements. The standard announcement format is usually followed. Although the full date is usually shown, some prefer to show just the month and the year.

Mr. and Mrs. Paul James Travis

announce the engagement of their daughter

Christina Lee

to

Mr. Allen Jay Fannin

February the fourteenth

Nineteen hundred and ninety-five

Bridal Thank-You Notes

A bride writes her thank-you notes on her own personalized stationery. She uses stationery with her own monogram or name on it. Since she is the only person writing the note, only her monogram or name should appear on the note. A dual monogram is not used. If the groom is going to be writing some of the thank-you notes, he should use his own personalized stationery.

The correct bridal thank-you note is a small ecru foldover note with the bride's initials engraved on the front. The monogram may be blind embossed or engraved in a conservative color. A blind embossed monogram is one in which the paper is raised but no ink is used.

The bride uses the initials representing her first name, maiden name, and married name. When all of the letters in the monogram are the same size, the initials appear in order. The monogram for Christina Travis Fannin reads "CTF." When the center initial is larger or highlighted, the initial representing the married name appears in the middle. Christina's initials then read "CFT."

Thank-You Notes Sent Before the Wedding

The bride will need thank-you notes to send before the wedding. Since she is not married, she must use notes showing initials representing her maiden name. If time does not allow her to order personalized notes, she may use blank notes. For a monogram in which all three initials are the same size the first, middle, and last names would appear in order. The monogram for Christina Lee Travis reads "CLT."

The middle letter represents the surname when it is larger than the other two letters. The monogram for Christina Lee Travis then reads "CTL."

Gift Received Cards

A bride sends gift received cards when she is going on a long honeymoon, or when she has a very large wedding and is unable to reply promptly. The cards acknowledge the receipt of the gift and promise that a personal thank-you will follow. Gift received cards are not sent in lieu of a personal thank-you note.

Mrs. Allen Jay Fanning

has received your very kind gift

and will write you later of her appreciation

GREETING CARDS,
SOCIAL ANNOUNCE-
MENTS, AND SOCIAL
CORRESPONDENCE

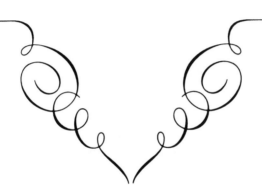

HOLIDAY CARDS

*H*oliday *cards* are mailed toward the end of the year by individuals and businesses. They may wish the recipient a "Happy Holiday," a "Happy Chanukah," or a "Merry Christmas." Cards sent by individuals may express a religious sentiment, but cards sent on behalf of a company should contain only a generic season's greeting.

You may personalize your holiday cards, so your name or the company's name appears with the greeting. Cards sent by a couple show the couple's first names followed by their surname. The woman's name appears first. Children's names appear beneath the parents' names.

The following are sample sentiments that you may wish to use.

MERRY CHRISTMAS

AND A

HAPPY NEW YEAR

THE O'NEAL FAMILY

Season's Greetings
and
Best Wishes for the New Year

Julie and Tom O'Neal
Patrick and Brian

Wishing you Joy and Happiness
during this Holiday Season
and throughout the New Year

Wishing you a joyous Christmas
with health and happiness
through the coming year

*May you find
health, happiness and peace
during this Holiday Season
and through the coming year*

1942

WITH CHRISTMAS GREETINGS

AND OUR BEST WISHES

FOR A

HAPPIER NEW YEAR

THE PRESIDENT

AND

MRS. ROOSEVELT

Jewish New Year Cards

Rosh Hashanah, the Jewish New Year, is one of the Jewish High Holidays. Yom Kippur, the day of atonement, occurs ten days after Rosh Hashanah.

Cards may be sent to wish family and friends a Happy New Year. The cards should be sent so that they are received before Rosh Hashanah.

Cards may be signed with first and last names or by the family. When using first names, the woman's name appears first. Children's names appear a line beneath the parents' names.

All good wishes

for health and happiness

through the coming year

Marian and Bill Goldstein

Jeffrey and Debbie

———————

MAY THE COMING

NEW YEAR

BRING YOU HEALTH AND HAPPINESS

THE GOLDSTEIN FAMILY

Birth Announcements

Parents may send a card to announce the birth of their child. The traditional birth announcement is a small card attached with a ribbon to a larger card. The small card shows the baby's name and date of birth. The larger card shows the names of the parents.

Birth announcements may also use a more standard format and read like a formal announcement. Of course, they may also be informal and imaginative.

If the baby's mother uses her maiden name and does not want to appear as "Mrs." on the birth announcement, her name appears on a separate line without a title.

Amy Krystine Romero
July the twenty-eighth
1995

Mr. and Mrs. John Paul Romero

Mr. and Mrs. John Paul Romero

announce the birth of their daughter

Amy Krystine

Monday, the twenty-eighth of July

1995

8 lbs., 12 ozs.

It's a Girl!!!

Margie and John Romero
joyfully proclaim
the birth of their daughter
Amy Krystine
July 28th, 1995

Mother Uses Maiden Name

Margie María Aponte
John Paul Romero
are pleased to announce
the birth of their daughter
Amy Krystine
July the twenty-eighth

1995

Twins

```
┌─────────────────────────────────────────────────────┐
│ ┌───────────────────┐   ┌───────────────────┐        │
│ │                   │   │                   │        │
│ │ Anna Elisabeth    │   │ Amy Krystine      │        │
│ │   Romero          │   │   Romero          │        │
│ │ July the          │   │ July the          │        │
│ │  twenty-eighth    │   │  twenty-eighth    │        │
│ │    1995           │   │    1995           │        │
│ │                   │   │                   │        │
│ └───────────────────┘   └───────────────────┘        │
│                                                       │
│                                                       │
│        Mr. and Mrs. John Paul Romero                  │
│                                                       │
│                                                       │
└─────────────────────────────────────────────────────┘
```

Adoption Announcements

Parents wishing to announce the adoption of an infant may use announcements similar to those used by parents to announce a birth. Sometimes the word "arrived" is substituted for "adoption." When the adoption of an older child involves a name change, the announcement should mention the change.

Patricia Susan Hamilton

Born May 23rd, 1995   *Arrived June 1st, 1995*

Mr. and Mrs. Martin Lewis Hamilton

Mr. and Mrs. Martin Lewis Hamilton
take pleasure in announcing that
Patricia Susan Hamilton
born on May 23rd, 1995
was adopted as their daughter
on June 1st, 1995

Mr. and Mrs. Donald Edward Chafee

take pleasure in announcing that

Jennifer Sue Foley

has been adopted as their daughter

and will hereafter be known as

Jennifer Sue Chafee

April 27th, 1993   *February 16th, 1995*

Christening Invitation

Christening invitations are usually informal. There is no standard format. Many times, they are engraved as a personal note.

Mr. and Mrs. James Patrick Smith

invite you

to the christening of their daughter

Stephanie

Sunday, the nineteenth of September

at eleven o'clock

Church of Saint Joseph

Seattle, Washington

Reception to follow at home

Stephanie will be christened on Sunday, the nineteenth of September at eleven o'clock at the Church of Saint Joseph. Please join us for this special occasion and for a small luncheon at our home after the service.

Denise and Jim Smith

Change of Address Announcements

A change of address announcement is sent to inform family and friends of a new address.

KAREN AND BILL SHEFFIELD

5310 CRIBARI GLEN

SAN JOSE, CALIFORNIA 95135

(408) 555-1212

We are now residing at

5310 Cribari Glen

San Jose, California 95135

Karen and Bill Sheffield

The new address of
Mr. and Mrs. William Sheffield
will be
5310 Cribari Glen
San Jose, California 95135
(408) 555~1212

Change of Name Announcements

People who decide to legally change their names may let others know by sending an announcement. The announcement is usually sent on a white or ecru card in black ink.

Mr. and Mrs. Henry Majchoretsky

announce that by permission of the court

they have taken the family name of

Majors

———————

Mrs. Roland Everett Peekskill

announces that she will resume the use

of her maiden name

and will now be known as

Linda Marie Trager

Thank-You Notes

Your appreciation of a gift should be acknowledged as soon after its receipt as possible. Your appreciation seems much more sincere when it is expressed promptly. Notes should be sent to thank someone for sending a gift, having you as a guest for dinner, or for any small favor. If you are unsure as to whether a thank-you note is called for, send one anyway. A note of appreciation is always welcome.

Thank-you notes are generally written on either a small foldover note or on a correspondence card. Although a woman may properly use either one, a man generally uses a correspondence card. The message is usually brief and generally consists of four parts:

1. The greeting.

Dear Barbara,

2. An appreciation of the item or favor.

Thank you for the beautiful, hand-carved walking stick.

3. Mention how useful it will be.

It's already a reliable companion on my daily constitutional.

4. Sign off with a suggestion of a future meeting.

I hope you'll find time to come up for a visit and to join us for a walk.

Love,
Dad

Dear Diane,
The book of magic tricks you gave me was greatly appreciated. It was a big hit with my niece and nephew. I look forward to seeing you soon.
Thanks again,
Steve

Dear Mr. and Mrs. Coronado,

The check you gave us for our wedding will come in handy. It will be a big help to us when we buy the CD player Tom and I have our eyes on. We hope to see you soon.

Sincerely,
Cathy

Memorial Service Invitations

A memorial service is given in memory of the deceased. It may be given any time after the funeral. The invitations are formal, usually black ink on a white or ecru letter sheet.

1903   *1995*

𝕴𝖓 𝖒𝖊𝖒𝖔𝖗𝖎𝖆𝖒

John Alexander Holmes

The honour of your presence
is requested at a memorial service
Wednesday, the twenty-first of January
at seven o'clock
First Methodist Church
Grove City, Pennsylvania

Condolence Notes

Condolence notes are letters of sympathy sent to the family of the deceased. They should be sent on a timely basis and should contain sincere expressions of sympathy. Condolence notes are sent at an obviously difficult time for the family so they should be brief. They should contain personal praise of the deceased and, if appropriate, mention how life was enriched because of him or her. Condolence notes should always end with an offer to be of service to the family.

Dear Tom;

    I was so sorry to hear about your father's death. I'll always remember playing ball with him in your backyard. He taught us to always give it our best. I'll miss him greatly.

    If there is anything I can do, please let me know.

                Sincerely,
                  Rich

Dear James;

    Michael and I are deeply saddened by Melissa's death. Good friends are hard to come by and Melissa was one of the best. We will sorely miss her friendship and love.

    Please call us if there is anything you need. We're always available.

                Love,
                Paula

Dear Mrs. Schwartzman;

 We were all surprised and saddened by your husband's death. Working for Mr. Schwartzman was a pleasure for all of us. His door was always open for us whenever we had a question or a problem.

 We hope that you'll continue to stop in to see us whenever you're in town.

Sincerely,
Susan Miller

Sympathy Acknowledgments

Sympathy acknowledgments should be handwritten notes of appreciation sent to family, friends, and business associates who have expressed their condolences. Engraved cards are sent only to those whom the family does not know personally, and then only when there is a large number of acknowledgments to be made. A personal message may be added to an engraved acknowledgment.

Sympathy acknowledgments may have a black border. At one time the width of the black border signified the sender's closeness to the deceased. Today many people choose not to use the black border. You may use a folded note or a flat card. Many people prefer a folded note, since it allows them to write a personal message on the inside.

The family of

Dr. Kenneth Parker Hamilton

acknowledges with grateful appreciation

your kind expression of sympathy

———————

We acknowledge with sincere thanks

the kind expression

of your sympathy

Mrs. Kenneth Parker and family

———————

During our time of sorrow
we learn how much our
friends mean to us
Your kindness and sympathy
will always be remembered
by the family of
Dr. Kenneth Hamilton Parker

THE FAMILY OF
DR. KENNETH HAMILTON PARKER
THANKS YOU SINCERELY
FOR YOUR KINDNESS AND SYMPATHY
AT A TIME WHEN IT WAS DEEPLY APPRECIATED

———————

Never are we more aware
of how much friends mean
than at the time of bereavement
Your thoughtfulness did so much
to ease our sorrow
The Parker Family

———————

Mrs. Kenneth Hamilton Parker
wishes to express her appreciation
and sincere thanks
for your kind expression
of sympathy

The Apostolic Delegate

deeply appreciates your participation

in the grief occasioned by the death of

His Holiness Pope Pius XI

and is sincerely grateful for your kind expression of sympathy

BUSINESS AND
PROFESSIONAL
STATIONERY

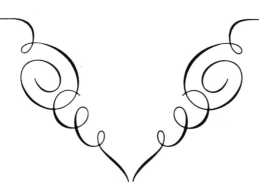

INTRODUCTION

Each letter written on business stationery is a personal emissary from one office to another. Corporate stationery influences the impression formed in the mind of the recipient, not only about the individual sender, but also about the company he or she represents. A high-quality cotton-fiber paper, a tasteful design, and quality engraving or thermography will create an image of elegance and distinction.

Corporate Letterhead

This 8½" x 11" sheet is used to identify, communicate, and project a corporate image. Information on the letterhead may include the firm's name, address, phone number, telex, and facsimile numbers. Letterheads for legal and professional firms often include a list of partners' names.

A partner or member of the firm may use the corporate letterhead with the corporate identity and his name and title. This sheet would be used only by that individual for his official business correspondence.

A letterhead without an individual's name and title is used by any member of the firm who is corresponding on behalf of the firm.

The corresponding envelopes show the corporate name and address on either the face or the back flap.

WEST COAST PROPERTIES, INC.
230 POWELL STREET
SAN FRANCISCO, CALIFORNIA 94102-1243

(415) 555-1212

CHARLES M. ALLERTON
PRESIDENT

WEST COAST PROPERTIES, INC.
230 POWELL STREET
SAN FRANCISCO, CALIFORNIA 94102-1243

(415) 555-1212

WEST COAST PROPERTIES
230 POWELL STREET
SAN FRANCISCO, CALIFORNIA 94102-1243

WEST COAST PROPERTIES
230 POWELL STREET
SAN FRANCISCO, CALIFORNIA 94102-1243

Monarch Sheets

Monarch sheets (7¼" x 10½") are used for personal business letters. They are used when writing a personal message on behalf of the firm or when writing a business letter to an associate who is on a first name basis with the sender. They may also be used as business letterheads by individuals engaged in professional services, such as doctors, lawyers, and consultants.

The name or the name and address appear on the sheet. When a monarch sheet is being used as corporate letterhead, the name, address, and phone number should appear. The envelope is imprinted with the name and address on the back flap.

CHARLES M. ALLERTON

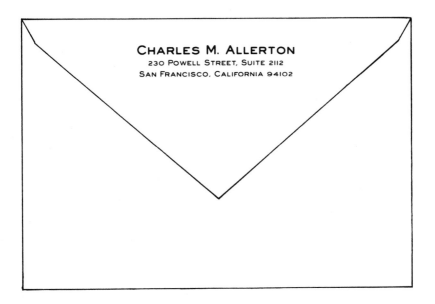

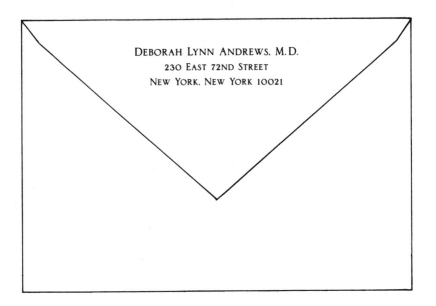

DEBORAH LYNN ANDREWS, M.D.
230 EAST 72ND STREET
NEW YORK, NEW YORK 10021

(212) 555-1212

Correspondence Cards

Correspondence cards are flat, heavy cards that are used for brief messages. Many business occasions and social business events should be followed by a short note or a written thank-you. A correspondence card allows you to write a brief personal note.

The executive's name appears at the top of the card. The envelope shows the name and address on the back flap.

CHARLES M. ALLERTON

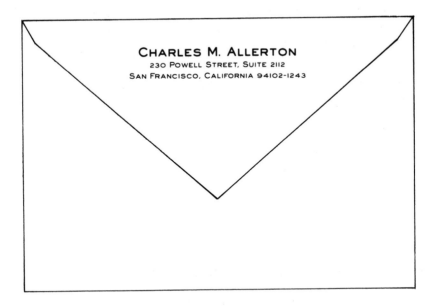

DEBORAH LYNN ANDREWS

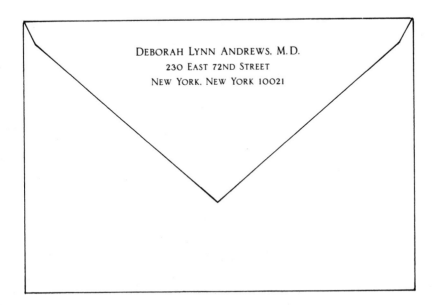

Business Cards

Business cards provide a client or a potential client with a means of contacting the presenter. The card should give all pertinent information neatly and concisely. It should be free from clutter.

A business card should be white or ecru and be imprinted with a black or grey ink. A standard size business card measures 3½" x 2". Members of less formal professions, such as artists and designers, may use more expressive cards, but professionals and business executives should stick to a conservative look.

CHARLES M. ALLERTON
PRESIDENT

WEST COAST PROPERTIES, INC.
230 POWELL STREET
SAN FRANCISCO, CALIFORNIA 94102   (415) 555-1212

DEBORAH LYNN ANDREWS, M.D.
OPHTHALMOLOGIST

230 EAST 72ND STREET   (212) 555-1212
NEW YORK, NEW YORK 10021   BY APPOINTMENT ONLY

Social Business Cards

Business cards should not be exchanged during social occasions. The use of a social business card is preferred. Social business cards are white or ecru with black or grey ink. Their standard size is 3½" x 2". The name and the business phone number appear on the card.

CHARLES M. ALLERTON

(415) 555-1212

DR. DEBORAH LYNN ANDREWS

(212) 555-1212

Message Cards

Message cards are used for any short messages. They are small cards (usually 3⁷⁄₁₆″ x 4⅞″ or 3¹¹⁄₁₆″ x 5⅛″) which have only a name or a name and title on them. They can be mailed in their corresponding envelopes or used within the company for interdepartmental messages.

They are often used as notes attached to items of interest that are being forwarded.

CHARLES M. ALLERTON
PRESIDENT

_____

WEST COAST PROPERTIES, INC.

CHARLES M. ALLERTON
PRESIDENT

_____

DEBORAH LYNN ANDREWS, M.D.

Business Invitations

Business invitations may be created for any type of function from a grand opening or relocation to a reception honoring retirees or top salesmen. They can be formal or informal, depending on the purpose of the event. The company's logo may be placed at the top of the invitation. As a courtesy to your guests, you may include with the invitation a card for your guests to give to their secretaries, letting them know how their bosses can be reached in case of an emergency.

It is impossible to include all types of business invitations in this book, but it should be possible to handle any situation by referring to the following samples.

MR. HERBERT SANDERS

REQUESTS THE PLEASURE OF YOUR COMPANY

AT A RECEPTION

TO INTRODUCE THE 1995 HOLIDAY LINE FOR

SHARON JAY TOGS

THURSDAY, THE THIRD OF FEBRUARY

AT EIGHT O'CLOCK

SHERATON CENTRE

NEW YORK

Mr. Wilfred D. Gillen

President, The Bell Telephone Company of Pennsylvania

The Diamond State Telephone Company

requests the pleasure of your company

at luncheon and a

Bell System Exhibit

demonstrating some of the latest developments

in communications and electronics

Friday, the thirtieth of September

at twelve-thirty o'clock

in the Hall of Honor

The Franklin Institute

Benjamin Franklin Parkway at Twentieth Street

Philadelphia, Pennsylvania

Please send response to
1835 Arch Street
Philadelphia 3, Pennsylvania

In honour of

Mr. Brian G. Downing

The Board of Directors

of

Southern Publishing Company, Inc.

requests the pleasure of your company

at dinner

Saturday, the twenty-first of October

at seven o'clock

Kiawah Island Inn and Resort

Kiawah Island, South Carolina

R. s. v. p.
Mrs. Raymond
(803) 555-1212

Black tie

To meet
Dr Edward Milton Potter

Dr Jennifer Susan Warren
Chairman, Valleyview Hospital Corp.
requests the pleasure of your company
at a cocktail reception
Thursday, the sixteenth of September
from six until eight o'clock
Hospitality Room, Valleyview Hospital
Minneapolis, Minnesota

Regrets only
Mrs Collins
(612) 555-1212

Invitation with Enclosure Card

Mr. Robert Chandler   Mr. Paul Morrison
Chairman of the Board   President

The Board of Directors

of

International Polymer, Inc.

request the pleasure of your company

at a dinner to celebrate their

One Hundredth Anniversary

Saturday, the eighteenth of April

at eight o'clock

The Metropolitan Museum of Art

New York

R. s. v. p.
Mary Lee Donovan
(212) 555-1212   Black tie

ENCLOSURE ENVELOPE

For your secretary

ENCLOSURE CARD

While attending
International Polymer's
dinner
I may be reached at
(212) 555-1212

Business Announcements

Announcements are sent to inform clients or other interested parties of a change in the status of a company. Announcements are made concerning a change of address, change of partners, introduction of a new officer, or the introduction of a new product.

Business announcements should be conservative unless the nature of the business allows for a creative look. Announcements are generally engraved in a conservative color on a white or ecru correspondence card.

It should be remembered that a company is a singular entity and that it requires the use of a singular verb. For example:

SIMPSON, HEALY INVESTMENTS, INC.

ANNOUNCES THAT ITS OFFICES

ETC.

and

Adamson and Shelton

is pleased to announce

etc.

Opening of an Office

LISA M. SIEGAL

CERTIFIED PUBLIC ACCOUNTANT

ANNOUNCES THE OPENING OF HER OFFICE

FOR THE PRACTICE OF TAX CONSULTING

1800 SOUTH TELEGRAPH ROAD

BLOOMFIELD HILLS, MICHIGAN

(313) 555-1212

———————

ROBERT LLOYD JENNINGS, M.D.

ANNOUNCES THE OPENING OF HIS OFFICE

FOR THE GENERAL PRACTICE OF MEDICINE

536 HIGH STREET

CHERRY HILL, NEW JERSEY

OFFICE HOURS
8:00 A.M. TO 6:00 P.M.
MONDAY THROUGH SATURDAY   (609) 555-1212

Miller, Morris and Matthews

is pleased to announce

the opening of their new

Miami Office

for the practice of immigration law

112 West 34th Street
New York, N. Y. 10001
(212) 555-1212

300 Biscayne Boulevard Way
Miami, Florida 33131
(305) 555-1212

Relocation of Offices

SIMPSON, HEALY INVESTMENTS, INC.

ANNOUNCES THAT ITS OFFICES

HAVE BEEN MOVED TO

200 HUNTINGTON AVENUE

BOSTON, MASSACHUSETTS

(617) 555-1212

Christopher G. McLain, M.D.

announces the relocation of his office to

The High Point Medical Center

325 Montlieu Avenue

High Point, North Carolina

(919) 555-1212

By appointment only

———

CUTTER INSURANCE AGENCY

IS PLEASED TO ANNOUNCE

THE REMOVAL OF THEIR OFFICES TO

399 MAPLEWOOD ROAD

LANCASTER, PENNSYLVANIA

(717) 555-1212

New Associate

Glenn P. Benoit

President, Benoit and Co.

takes pleasure in announcing that

Angelyn Marlette

has joined the company as

Vice President, Legal Services

3500 Northwestern Avenue
Racine, Wisconsin 53405

(414) 555-1212

Blake T. Griffen

Chairman

Triad Cable Co., Inc.

is pleased to announce that

Richard Allen Reynolds

has been named

Senior Vice President, Southwest Region

2000 Massachusetts Avenue, N.W.
Washington, D.C. 20008
(202) 555-1212

1700 Commerce Street
Fort Worth, Texas 76102
(817) 555-1212

Admittance of a New Partner

Adamson and Shelton

Attorneys at Law

is pleased to announce that

David S. Clifford

has been admitted to the partnership

The firm name will now be known as

Adamson, Shelton and Clifford

1300 Walnut Street
Philadelphia, Pennsylvania 19107

(215) 555-1212

Formation of a Partnership

Brian R. Toomey

and

Henry T. Warren

announce the formation of a partnership

for the general practice of law

under the firm name of

Toomey and Warren

725 Rio Grande Boulevard, N.W.
Albuquerque, New Mexico 87104

(505) 555-1212

Announcement of a Death

The Officers and Directors

of

Kensington Manufacturing Company, Inc.

announce with deep regret the death of

Phillip T. Kensington, Jr.

on Monday, the nineteenth of October

Nineteen hundred and ninety~five

Résumés

Think of your résumé as sales promotion material. Its product is you, and its purpose is to sell you to a prospective employer. When you are selling yourself (or anything for that matter), always mention the positive, never the negative. Your cup is always half full, never half empty. You should always be honest, but honesty should not prevent you from presenting yourself in a positive light. Your prospective employer wants someone who will be an asset to the company. Your résumé needs to convince them that you will be an asset.

The executive who receives your résumé will, no doubt, be busy. Your résumé needs to capture and hold your prospective employer's interest. Do not waste his or her time. Make your résumé concise and easy to read. Try to limit it to one page.

Your résumé should look professional and appealing. Use a 100-percent cotton-fiber paper. The quality of the paper will make your résumé stand out from your competition's résumés. It should be neatly typed and laid out. If you need to hire someone to type it for you to achieve that look, do it. It is a good investment. Your résumé will not sell you if it does not look professional.

Your résumé should contain any information that would be important to a prospective employer. It should have your name, address, and phone number at the top. A statement of your career objective may follow. The two major sections of your résumé are "Work Experience" and "Education." You list whichever section would be of the most interest to your prospective employer first. That section will sell you best. If you have been working for several years, you should present your work experience first, since your prospective employer will want to know what you have accomplished for other companies. Recent college graduates should present their educational experience first, since their education is more important than the jobs they held while working their way through college.

Your work experience should be presented in reverse chronological order. Your job title, employer, employer's name and address, and a concise description of your responsibilities and achievements should be given for each employer.

Educational information should include the name of the high school or college that you last attended. You should list any degrees, certificates, and honors that you achieved.

You may include personal information on your résumé such as marital information, weight, and height. This information is entirely optional. You may also include a list of the activities in which you participate. If you include activities on your résumé, mention how those experiences have helped to develop you into the kind of person your prospective employer would want to hire. You should have a list of available references for your prospective employer, and you may add a line at the end of your résumé stating that your references are available upon request.

WARREN L. MALIC
3015 Fontana Drive
Houston, Texas   77043
(713) 555-1212

PROFESSIONAL EXPERIENCE

July 1992–Present	Communications Specialist. Major Accounts Program. Western Communications, Inc. 1210 Allen Center, Houston, Texas
	Responsibilities: Customer Relations, Traffic Analysis/Service Consultation, Customer Revenue, and Account Maintenance.
	Accomplishments: Created Division's first PC based install and revenue tracking system. Installed Division's first VNET and 800 services. Received five CSC awards.
September 1989–July 1992	Telemarketing Sales Halstead Communications, Inc.
August 1985–September 1989	Social Studies Teacher: Secondary Level Lamar Consolidated Independent School System Rosenberg, Texas

EDUCATION

June 1991–May 1994	University of Houston Houston, Texas
	Course concentration: Masters of Administration and supervision.
September 1985	Dowling College Oakdale, New York
	Bachelor of Arts in Social Science

REFERENCES

Available upon request

200

KATHLEEN M. PACE
1400 Orchard Street
Alexandria, VA   22302
(703) 555-1212

CAREER OBJECTIVE

A position of responsibility in the field of marketing.

EDUCATION

University of Virginia
Charlottesville, VA   22903

May 1995

B.B.A. in Marketing
Graduated Magna Cum Laude
Student Government Treasurer
Minored in Spanish, spent junior year in Spain.

WORK EXPERIENCE

September 1993–May 1995

University of Virginia
Charlottesville, VA   22903
Education Department
Taught English as a second language during the school year.

June–August 1993

Smithsonian Institute
Washington, DC   20560
Assisted Director of Children's Programs

September 1992–May 1993

University of Virginia
Charlottesville, VA   22903
Spanish Tutor
Tutored students in Spanish as part of work study program.

June–August 1992

Walt Disney World
Lake Buena Vista, Florida   32830
Official Greeter

June–August 1989–1991

Hickory Bill's Barbeque
115 King Street
Alexandria, VA   22302
Waitress

REFERENCES

Available upon request

201

Cover Letters

Like résumés, cover letters sell you to a prospective employer. Their purpose is to create enough of an interest in you to convince the prospective employer to read your résumé and grant you an interview. Your cover letter should let your prospective employer know that hiring you will benefit the company.

The first paragraph of your cover letter should attract your prospective employer's interest. If you know somebody at the company, mention his or her name. This will catch the reader's eye, and he or she will be more likely to follow up on your request for an interview. Many companies like to hire people who are recommended to them by their employees.

Go to the library and research the company to which you apply. Read their annual report and their evaluation in *Standard and Poor's, Value Line,* or other business publications that evaluate many publicly traded companies. They contain a wealth of information you can use in your cover letter and your interview.

Tailor your cover letter to the needs and interests of that company. The person who reads your cover letter is probably a dedicated employee. Flatter the prospective employer by mentioning something positive about the company (something you picked up in your research). Tell them why you want to work for their company.

Your cover letter should convince its reader that you will be an asset to the company. Highlight your qualificatons. Tell your prospective employer how valuable your experience, education, and achievements are, and how you will use them to benefit the company.

End your letter with a request for an interview and a method for contacting you.

Remember to be concise and professional. Your cover letter should make you look competent. Use the best available paper, and make sure it is typed neatly and accurately. The statement made by the appearance of your cover letter is as important as that made by the words themselves.

3015 Fontana Drive
Houston, Texas   77043

October 5, 1995

Mr. Stuart B. Russell
Clinton Telecommunicatins, Inc.
3115 Commerce, Suite 1701
Houston, Texas   77002

Dear Mr. Russell:

Ms. Julie Stephens suggested that I contact you regarding the position as manager of your customer service department. My three years experience at WCI as Communications Specialist in charge of major accounts will be valuable in keeping Clinton Telecommunicatons a leader in the long distance-communications field.

At WCI, I received five customer service citations while installing our division's first VNET and 800 service and our first install and revenue tracking system. I am confident that my expertise, my organizational skills, and my self-confidence will prove an asset for Clinton Telecommunications.

I look forward to meeting you to discuss my employment opportunities. I may be contacted at (713) 555-1212.

Sincerely,

Warren L. Malic

Follow-up Thank-You Letter

You will stand out from the crowd of interviewees when you send a personal thank-you letter to the person who interviewed you. This gesture will tell the interviewer that you are well-mannered and appreciative.

The thank-you note is an opportunity to display more than just your good manners. It is another opportunity to sell yourself.

Thank the interviewer for his or her time. Mention your continued interest in the position and reemphasize the attributes that you will bring to that position. When you are writing the thank-you letter, you have a better idea of what the company is looking for. Use that knowledge to your advantage. Close your letter with a request for further communication.

3015 *Fontana Drive*
Houston, Texas 77043

October 26, 1995

Mr. Stuart B. Russell
Clinton Telecommunicatins, Inc.
3115 Commerce, Suite 1701
Houston, Texas 77002

Dear Mr. Russell:

I appreciate your meeting with me yesterday. I am excited about the possibility of heading your customer service department.

The skills and contacts that I developed while working with WCI's major accounts will greatly assist me at Clinton Telecommunications.

Thank you again for your time. I look forward to hearing from you in the near future.

Sincerely,

Warren L. Malic

CALLING CARDS

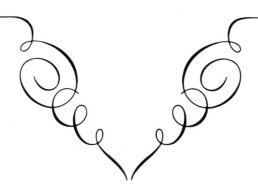

THE HISTORY OF CALLING CARDS

In Europe, the first known use of a calling card occurred in Italy during the latter part of the sixteenth century. The custom spread to France, Great Britain, and eventually America.

Calling cards were originally made for the nobility to hand to a footman when paying a call or to leave at the home when the person called upon was absent. Their use was popularized during the reign of Louis XVI when the custom developed in France to use them when paying New Year's calls.

Calligraphers made the early calling cards, which bore the name of the individual and his hereditary titles. The cards were further embellished with borders, flower designs, and other ornamentations. Early in the nineteenth century, these embellishments were abandoned in favor of a fine card on which only the individual's name was engraved.

When making a social call, you leave a calling card for each adult on whom you are calling, never, however, exceeding three cards. A man may call on a husband and wife, so he leaves two cards. A woman may only call on another woman, so she leaves only one card. You may turn down the corner of your card to signify that it is intended for all the ladies of the house.

Calling cards are still used for their original purpose, but are now more often used as gift enclosures. To personalize the gift enclosure, a line is drawn through the engraving and a brief handwritten message and/or signature is added.

Calling cards are available in several sizes. The sizes indicate male or female, married or single. The following are the correct sizes for use by individuals and couples issuing joint cards:

Child	2¼″ x 1⅜″
Single Woman	2⅞″ x 2″
Married Woman	3⅛″ x 2¼″
Man	3⅜″ x 1½″ or 3½″ x 2″
Married Couple	3⅜″ x 2½″

Calling Cards for Men

Men's Cards

A man's full name is always used, preceded by his title, that is, Mr., Dr., Colonel. His name may be followed by Jr., III, etc. On a calling card, "junior" may be abbreviated as it will balance better with "Mr." Depending on one's preference, a comma may or may not precede II or III.

Mr. Griffen Alexander Greylock

Mr. Griffen Alexander Greylock, Jr.

Mr. Griffen Alexander Greylock, III

Mr. Griffen Alexander Greylock III

Boys' Cards

A title does not precede the name of a boy under the age of eighteen.

Thomas Arthur Hancock

Calling Cards for Women

Married Women

A married woman uses her husband's full name, prefaced by "Mrs." Her street address, without the city and state, may be shown in the lower right-hand corner when she lives in a large town. If she lives in the suburbs or the country, the city and state should also appear.

Mrs. Harrison Raiford Booth

or

Mrs. Harrison Raiford Booth

211 East 79th Street

SUFFIXES

The same suffix that appears on a husband's card appears on the wife's card.

Mrs. Harrison Raiford Booth, Jr.

Widows

A widow continues to use her husband's name on her calling card. When her married son no longer uses "junior," she must use the suffix "senior" to distinguish her from her daughter-in-law.

Mrs. Harrison Raiford Booth

Mrs. Harrison Raiford Booth, senior

Divorced Women

Traditionally, a divorced woman who retained her married name after her divorce engraved her calling cards with "Mrs." followed by her maiden and married names. Today, a divorced woman may, if she prefers, use "Mrs." followed by her first, maiden, and married names.

Mrs. Renner Booth

Mrs. Lydia Renner Booth

A title should not be used when a divorced woman resumes the use of her maiden name.

Lydia Anne Renner

The Use of "Ms."

"Ms." should not appear on calling cards. If a woman feels uncomfortable using "Miss" or "Mrs.," she may properly omit her title.

SINGLE WOMAN

Lydia Anne Renner

MARRIED OR DIVORCED WOMAN

Lydia Renner Booth

Single Women

A single woman typically uses her full name preceded by "Miss." However, she may, if she prefers, show only her full name.

Miss Lydia Anne Renner

or

Lydia Anne Renner

Mr. and Mrs.

A calling card used jointly by a husband and wife has "Mr. and Mrs." followed by the husband's full name engraved on it. If the husband has a title other than "Mr.," that title is used instead. The wife should use "Mrs." as that is her correct social title. The street address without the city and state may appear in the lower right-hand corner when the husband and wife reside in a large town. If they live in the suburbs or the country, the town and state should be included in the address.

Titles, except "Mr.," "Mrs.," and "Dr.," should not be abbreviated. When a name is too long to fit on a calling card, it is preferable to omit the middle name rather than to abbreviate a title or use an initial.

Mr. and Mrs. Harrison Raiford Booth

Dr. and Mrs. Harrison Raiford Booth

The Reverend and Mrs. Harrison Booth

Medical Doctors

Physicians, surgeons, and dentists use the prefix "Doctor" or "Dr." on their calling cards. Professional degrees should not appear on cards for social use.

A single woman who is a medical doctor or a married woman who has retained her maiden name or uses a professional name prefaces her full name with "Doctor" or "Dr."

A married woman who is a doctor and uses her husband's name engraves her husband's name preceded by "Mrs." on her calling cards. She may, of course, use her own married name professionally, in which case her calling card shows her first, maiden, and married names, preceded by "Doctor" or "Dr."

Man

DOCTOR JEFFREY ALLEN GLENNWOOD

or

DR. JEFFREY ALLEN GLENNWOOD

Single Woman

Doctor Leslie Jean Carpenter

or

Dr. Leslie Jean Carpenter

Married Woman

Mrs. Frederick Winthrop Hollings

or

Doctor Leslie Carpenter Hollings

or

Dr. Leslie Carpenter Hollings

University and College Titles

Calling cards for general social use for college and university faculty members show no academic titles. Letters indicating advanced degrees do not appear.

However, calling cards for college and university use may show academic titles. The titles are never abbreviated. If there is not enough room on the card because of a long name, the middle name may be omitted. Letters indicating advanced degrees do not appear.

General Social Use

MR. GREGORY WINSTON HUGHES

College and University Use

PROFESSOR GREGORY HUGHES

Clergy

Members of the clergy use their full names preceded by their title on social calling cards. Titles are never abbreviated. The middle name may be omitted if there is not enough space on the card. No initials indicating divinity degrees appear on the card.

Rabbi Nathan Weisman

The Reverend Kenneth Rhoads

Government Officials

Calling cards for the President, the Vice President, the Speaker of the House, and members of the Cabinet are engraved with just the official's title. The official's name does not appear on calling cards.

The President

The Vice President

The Speaker of the House

The Secretary of State

Joint calling cards for government officials and their wives other than the President and his wife show the office followed by "and Mrs. James Driggs." Joint cards for the President and his wife read:

*The President
and Mrs. Washington*

The cards for the wife of the President would read:

Mrs. Washington

The cards for the wives of the Vice President, the Speaker of the House, and the members of the Cabinet should read "Mrs." followed by their husband's full name.

Mrs. John Quincy Adams

Supreme Court Justices

The Chief Justice of the United States Supreme Court shows only his title on his calling card.

THE CHIEF JUSTICE

Calling cards for an Associate Justice of the Supreme Court show "Mr. (or Madam) Justice" followed by the Justice's surname.

MR. JUSTICE MARSHALL

JUDGES IN OTHER COURTS

Judges in courts other than the Supreme Court use their full name prefaced by "Judge" on their calling cards.

JUDGE ALEXANDRA LEE BLACK

Joint calling cards and calling cards for spouses of judges follow the same guidelines as those for other government officials.

United States Senator

JENNIFER ANN HANSEN

UNITED STATES SENATE   MASSACHUSETTS

United States Representative

James Lawrence Pendleton

United States   **Third District**
House of Representatives   **Pennsylvania**

Governor of a State

The name of the governor of a state appears above the office in the center of a calling card. When the office rather than the individual is being represented, only the office is shown.

Paula Jean Magnuson

Governor of California

or

The Governor of California

State Senators and Representatives

State senators and representatives use the same card as they would in private life.

Mayor

A mayor's social card is the same as that used in private life. The official card has the mayor's name with the office beneath the name.

When the office rather than the individual is being represented, only the office is shown.

Mr. Jorge LaGuerella

Jorge LaGuerella
Mayor of Miami

The Mayor of Miami

Military

Calling cards are used frequently in the military. They are used for making calls and as gift enclosures. When an officer is assigned to a new post, he calls on his commanding officer. Cards used by the military are the same size as civilian cards: male officer, 3⅛" x 1½" or 3½" x 2"; single female officer, 2⅞" x 2"; married female officer, 3⅛" x 2¼"; joint cards, 3⅜" x 2½".

In the Navy and Coast Guard, officers with the rank of commander and above use their titles preceding their names. Their branch of service appears in the lower right-hand corner of the card. Officers with the rank of vice admiral and above may use just their title and surname, while officers below that rank use their full name.

Junior officers show only their full name in the center of the card. Their rank and service designation appear in the lower right-hand corner. Midshipmen use the same format as junior officers. Below the rank of ensign, the name appears in the center of the card. The service designation appears in the lower right-hand corner. Their rank does not appear.

In the Army, Air Force, and Marines, officers with the rank of major and above may preface their names with their titles. Their service designation appears in the lower right-hand corner. Officers with the rank of major general and above may use just their rank and surname, while officers below that rank use their full names.

Company grade officers and cadets in the United States Military Academy show only their full names in the center of the card. Their rank and service designation appear in the lower right-hand corner. First lieutenants and second lieutenants both use "Lieutenant." Non-commissioned officers and cadets may also use this format. Members of the Army with a rank below sergeant use their names in the center of the card and their branch of service in the lower right-hand corner. Their rank does not appear.

Calling cards for retired officers in any branch of service show the word "Retired" beneath the service designation. "Retired" is not used on a joint card for a retired officer and his wife.

General Frederickson

United States Army

Colonel William Warren Hudson

United States Marine Corps
Retired

Colonel and Mrs William Warren Hudson

SUSAN DIANE STRICKLAND

LIEUTENANT
UNITED STATES AIR FORCE

———————

PAUL CARLOS RIVERA

MASTER SERGEANT
UNITED STATES ARMY

———————

Leonard Arnold Pfister

United States Navy

———————

Jennifer Sue Stone

Cadet
United States Military Academy

8

APPENDIX

FORMS OF ADDRESS

The President of the United States

SALUTATION: Dear Mr. (Madam) President,

CLOSING: Most respectfully yours,

INVITATION, MAN: The President and Mrs. Washington
WOMAN: The President and Mr. Washington

SOCIAL ENVELOPE, MAN: The President and Mrs. Washington
WOMAN: The President and Mr. Washington

OFFICIAL ENVELOPE: The President
The White House
Washington, D.C.   20500

Former President of the United States

SALUTATION: Dear Mr. (Mrs.) Jefferson,

CLOSING: Sincerely yours,

INVITATION: Mr. and Mrs. Thomas Jefferson

SOCIAL ENVELOPE, MAN: The Honorable Thomas Jefferson
and Mrs. Jefferson
WOMAN: The Honorable Joan Jefferson
and Mr. Jefferson

OFFICIAL ENVELOPE: The Honorable Thomas Jefferson

The Vice President of the United States

SALUTATION: Dear Mr. (Madam) Vice President,

CLOSING: Sincerely yours,

INVITATION, MAN: The Vice President and Mrs. Adams
WOMAN: The Vice President and Mr. Adams

SOCIAL ENVELOPE, MAN: The Vice President and Mrs. Adams
WOMAN: The Vice President and Mr. Adams

OFFICIAL ENVELOPE: The Vice President
United States Senate
Washington, D.C.   20510

Cabinet Member

SALUTATION: Dear Mr. (Madam) Secretary,

CLOSING: Sincerely yours,

INVITATION, MAN: The Secretary of State and Mrs. Novak
WOMAN: The Secretary of State and Mr. Novak

SOCIAL ENVELOPE, MAN: The Secretary of State and
Mrs. Novak
WOMAN: The Secretary of State and Mr. Novak

OFFICIAL ENVELOPE: The Honorable William Novak
Secretary of State
Washington, D.C.   20520

Attorney General

SALUTATION: Dear Mr. (Madam) Attorney General,

CLOSING: Sincerely yours,

INVITATION, MAN: The Attorney General and Mrs. Sharrer
WOMAN: The Attorney General and Mr. Sharrer

SOCIAL ENVELOPE, MAN: The Attorney General and
Mrs. Sharrer
WOMAN: The Attorney General and
Mr. Sharrer

OFFICIAL ENVELOPE: The Honorable Robert Sharrer
Attorney General
Washington, D.C.   20530

United States Senator

SALUTATION: Dear Senator Collins,

CLOSING: Sincerely yours,

INVITATION, MAN: Senator Stephen Collins or
Mr. and Mrs. Stephen Collins
WOMAN: Senator Margaret Collins or
Mr. and Mrs. Stephen Collins

SOCIAL ENVELOPE, MAN: The Honorable Stephen Collins
and Mrs. Collins
WOMAN: The Honorable Margaret Collins
and Mr. Collins

OFFICIAL ENVELOPE: The Honorable Margaret Collins
United States Senate
Washington, D.C.   20510

The Speaker of the House of Representatives

SALUTATION: Dear Mr. (Madam) Speaker,

CLOSING: Sincerely yours,

INVITATION, MAN: The Speaker of the House and
Mrs. Barscz or
The Speaker and Mrs. Barscz
WOMAN: The Speaker of the House and Mr. Barscz or
The Speaker and Mr. Barscz

SOCIAL ENVELOPE, MAN: The Speaker of the House and
Mrs. Barscz
WOMAN: The Speaker of the House and
Mr. Barscz

OFFICIAL ENVELOPE: The Honorable Joyce Barscz
Speaker of the House of Representatives
The Capitol
Washington, D.C.   20515

Member of the House of Representatives

SALUTATION: Dear Mr. (Mrs.) Covington,

CLOSING: Sincerely yours,

INVITATION: Mr. and Mrs. Samuel Covington

SOCIAL ENVELOPE, MAN: The Honorable Samuel Covington
and Mrs. Covington
WOMAN: The Honorable Jean Covington
and Mr. Covington

OFFICIAL ENVELOPE: The Honorable Samuel Covington
House of Representatives
Washington, D.C.   20515

The Chief Justice of the Supreme Court

SALUTATION: Dear Mr. (Madam) Chief Justice,

CLOSING: Sincerely yours,

INVITATION, MAN: The Chief Justice and Mrs. Holmes
WOMAN: The Chief Justice and Mr. Holmes

SOCIAL ENVELOPE, MAN: The Chief Justice and Mrs. Holmes
WOMAN: The Chief Justice and Mr. Holmes

OFFICIAL ENVELOPE: The Chief Justice of the Supreme Court
Washington, D.C.   20543

Associate Justice of the Supreme Court

SALUTATION: Dear Mr. (Madam) Justice,

CLOSING: Sincerely yours,

INVITATION, MAN: Mr. Justice Gladstone and Mrs. Gladstone
WOMAN: Madam Justice Gladstone and Mr. Gladstone

SOCIAL ENVELOPE, MAN: Mr. Justice Gladstone and
Mrs. Gladstone
WOMAN: Madam Justice Gladstone and
Mr. Gladstone

OFFICIAL ENVELOPE: Mr. (Madam) Justice Gladstone
The Supreme Court
Washington, D.C.   20543

United States Ambassador to the United Nations

SALUTATION: Dear Mr. (Madam) Ambassador,

CLOSING: Sincerely yours,

INVITATION: Mr. and Mrs. Donald Eisemann

SOCIAL ENVELOPE, MAN: The United States Representative to the
United Nations and Mrs. Eisemann
WOMAN: The United States Representative to the
United Nations and Mr. Eisemann

OFFICIAL ENVELOPE: The Honorable Donald Eisemann
The United States Representative
to the United Nations
United Nations Plaza
New York, NY   10017

American Ambassador

SALUTATION: Dear Mr. (Madam) Ambassador,

CLOSING: Sincerely yours,

INVITATION: Mr. and Mrs. Harold Dickey

SOCIAL ENVELOPE, MAN: The Ambassador of the United States and Mrs. Dickey
WOMAN: The Ambassador of the United States and Mr. Dickey

OFFICIAL ENVELOPE: The Honorable Harold Dickey
The Ambassador of the United States
Tokyo, Japan

Secretary General of the United Nations

SALUTATION: Dear Mr. (Madam) Secretary General,

CLOSING: Sincerely yours,

INVITATION, MAN: The Secretary General of the United Nations and Mrs. Venezia
WOMAN: The Secretary General of the United Nations and Mr. Venezia

SOCIAL ENVELOPE, MAN: His Excellency, The Secretary General of the United Nations and Mrs. Venezia
WOMAN: Her Excellency, The Secretary General of the United Nations and Mr. Venezia

OFFICIAL ENVELOPE: His (Her) Excellency,
The Secretary General of the
United Nations
United Nations Plaza
New York, NY   10017

Foreign Ambassador

SALUTATION: Dear Mr. (Madam) Ambassador,

CLOSING: Sincerely yours,

INVITATION, MAN: The Ambassador of Spain
and Mrs. Orlando
WOMAN: The Ambassador of Spain
and Mr. Orlando

SOCIAL ENVELOPE, MAN: His Excellency, The Ambassador of
Spain and Mrs. Orlando
WOMAN: Her Excellency, The Ambassador of
Spain and Mr. Orlando

OFFICIAL ENVELOPE: His (Her) Excellency Juan Orlando
Ambassador of Spain

Governor

SALUTATION: Dear Governor Clinton,

CLOSING: Sincerely yours,

INVITATION, MAN: The Governor of New York and
Mrs. Clinton
WOMAN: The Governor of New York and
Mr. Clinton

SOCIAL ENVELOPE, MAN: The Governor and Mrs. Clinton
WOMAN: The Governor and Mr. Clinton

OFFICIAL ENVELOPE: The Honorable George Clinton
Governor of New York

State Senator or Representative

SALUTATION: Dear Mr. (Mrs.) Flanagan,

CLOSING: Sincerely yours,

INVITATION: Mr. and Mrs. John Flanagan

SOCIAL ENVELOPE, MAN: The Honorable John Flanagan
and Mrs. Flanagan
WOMAN: The Honorable Mary Flanagan
and Mr. Flanagan

OFFICIAL ENVELOPE: The Honorable John Flanagan

Mayor

SALUTATION: Dear Mayor Santiago,

CLOSING: Sincerely yours,

INVITATION, MAN: The Mayor of Santa Fe
and Mrs. Santiago
WOMAN: The Mayor of Sante Fe
and Mr. Santiago

SOCIAL ENVELOPE, MAN: The Honorable Paul Santiago
and Mrs. Santiago
WOMAN: The Honorable Carla Santiago
and Mr. Santiago

OFFICIAL ENVELOPE: The Honorable Carla Santiago

Judge

SALUTATION: Dear Judge Knapp,

CLOSING: Sincerely yours,

INVITATION, MAN: Judge and Mrs. Harold Knapp
WOMAN: Mr. and Mrs. Harold Knapp

BOTH ARE JUDGES: The Judges Knapp

The Pope

SALUTATION: Your Holiness, or Most Holy Father,

CLOSING: Your most humble servant,

ENVELOPE: His Holiness Pope John Paul II

Cardinal

SALUTATION: Your Eminence, or Dear Cardinal McGrath,

CLOSING: Your humble servant,

ENVELOPE: His Eminence, John Cardinal McGrath

Archbishop

SALUTATION: Your Excellency, or Dear Archbishop Daley,

CLOSING: Your obedient servant,

ENVELOPE: The Most Reverend Francis Xavier Daley

Bishop

SALUTATION: Most Reverend Sir, or Dear Bishop Carlucci,

CLOSING: Your obedient servant,

ENVELOPE: The Most Reverend Peter Carlucci

Abbot

SALUTATION: Right Reverend Johnson, or Dear Father Johnson,

CLOSING: Your obedient servant,

ENVELOPE: The Right Reverend Laurence Johnson

Monsignor

SALUTATION: Right Reverend Monsignor, or Dear Monsignor
LaRue,

CLOSING: Yours faithfully,

ENVELOPE: The Right Reverend Monsignor Stephen LaRue

Priest

SALUTATION: Reverend Father, or Dear Father O'Malley,

CLOSING: Yours faithfully,

ENVELOPE: The Reverend Father Patrick O'Malley

Brother

SALUTATION: Dear Brother Andrew,

CLOSING: Yours faithfully,

ENVELOPE: Brother Andrew, (initials of his order)

Mother Superior

SALUTATION: Dear Reverend Mother,

CLOSING: Yours faithfully,

ENVELOPE: The Reverend Mother Emily

Sister

SALUTATION: Dear Sister Mary,

CLOSING: Yours faithfully,

ENVELOPE: Sister Mary, (initials of her order)

Episcopal Bishop

SALUTATION: Right Reverend Sir, or Dear Bishop,

CLOSING: Sincerely yours,

SOCIAL ENVELOPE: The Right Reverend and Mrs. Leland Osgood

OFFICIAL ENVELOPE: The Right Reverend Leland Osgood, D.D. Bishop of Philadelphia

Protestant Clergy

SALUTATION: Dear Mr. (Mrs.) Stapleton,

CLOSING: Sincerely yours,

INVITATION, MAN: The Reverend and Mrs. James Stapleton
WOMAN: Mr. and Mrs. James Stapleton

SOCIAL ENVELOPE, MAN: The Reverend and Mrs. James Stapleton
WOMAN: Mr. and Mrs. James Stapleton

OFFICIAL ENVELOPE: The Reverend Lucille Stapleton

Protestant Clergy with Doctorate

SALUTATION: Dear Dr. Kingston,

CLOSING: Sincerely yours,

INVITATION, MAN: The Reverend Dr. and Mrs. Frederic Kingston
WOMAN: Mr. and Mrs. Frederic Kingston

SOCIAL ENVELOPE, MAN: The Reverend Dr. and Mrs. Frederic Kingston
WOMAN: Mr. and Mrs. Frederic Kingston

OFFICIAL ENVELOPE: The Reverend Dr. Linda Kingston

Rabbi

SALUTATION: Dear Rabbi Levine,

CLOSING: Sincerely yours,

INVITATION: Rabbi and Mrs. Daniel Levine

SOCIAL ENVELOPE: Rabbi and Mrs. Daniel Levine

OFFICIAL ENVELOPE: Rabbi Daniel Levine

Rabbi with Doctorate

SALUTATION: Dear Rabbi Feldman, or Dear Dr. Feldman,

CLOSING: Sincerely yours,

INVITATION: Rabbi and Mrs. Stanley Feldman or
Dr. and Mrs. Stanley Feldman

SOCIAL ENVELOPE: Rabbi (Dr.) and Mrs. Stanley Feldman

OFFICIAL ENVELOPE: Rabbi Stanley Feldman

ABOUT CRANE AND CO., INC.

In 1776, the Massachusetts Bay Colony issued the first colonial bank notes that were backed by a colony and not by the English Crown. Stephen Crane's mill produced the paper for those bank notes and sold them to Paul Revere. Although better known for his midnight ride, Paul Revere engraved those first colonial bank notes.

In 1799, Stephen's son, Zenas Crane, headed west to search for a site for a mill of his own. He needed a place with an abundant supply of fresh water (for power and for cleansing the rags used in papermaking) and where the surrounding area would produce both an ample supply of rags for use as a raw material and a growing market. (Housewives saved their rags and sold them or bartered them to the general store. A rag merchant bought the rags and resold them to the paper mill, where they were transformed into paper.)

Zenas Crane's search ended in Dalton, Massachusetts, a small agricultural community nestled in the Berkshire Hills. Dalton's location gave him the water he needed and access to southern markets through New York City and western markets through Albany, New York.

In partnership with John Willard and Henry Wiswall, Zenas Crane purchased a fourteen-acre site for the sum of $194. Crane & Co.,

Inc. was founded in 1801 when the new company placed an advertisement in the *Pittsfield Sun* asking ladies to sell them their rags.

Zenas Crane's company produced paper for businesses, printers, and publishers. He also sold paper to the independent banks that were authorized to print paper money.

Bond paper is a paper with a hard finish that is used for bonds, stock certificates, and business letterheads. The term was first used in 1850 when the president of a New York bank wrote to Crane asking for some "bond paper." The term soon became the generic term for the type of paper used for bonds.

Also at that time, paper money was being counterfeited by a process called raising the money, which was the illegal process of changing, for example, a one dollar bill into a ten dollar bill, by drawing a zero after the one on the bill. In 1844, Crane developed a technique to put silk threads in its bank-note paper to prevent the raising of money. Crane put a single thread in one dollar bills, two threads in two dollar bills, and three threads in three dollar bills. If somebody held what appeared to be a ten dollar bill to the light and saw a single silk thread, he knew that the bill was counterfeit.

Crane's mastering of this innovative technique was instrumental in the company's landing a contract in 1879 to supply the paper for the currency of the United States. Since that day, Crane has supplied virtually all U.S. currency paper to the United States Bureau of Engraving and Printing. Crane also supplies currency and bank-note paper to the governments of some forty other countries.

The company Zenas Crane founded in 1801 has grown, prospered, and diversified but is still owned by his descendants, still makes 100-percent cotton-fiber papers, and still adheres to the quality standards on which he insisted.

Crane products today include currency and security papers, ledger and record papers, architectural and engineering drafting papers, nonwoven technical products, and a complete line of business and social stationery papers for corporate letterheads, social correspondence, and wedding invitations.

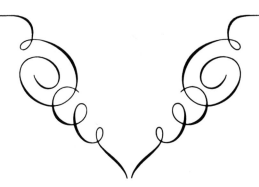

ACKNOWLEDGMENTS

The following illustrations are from the collection of the Crane Museum of Papermaking:

Page 33:   Invitation to a dinner in honor of Winston Churchill (1949).

Page 36:   Invitation to a reception in honor of Princess Elizabeth (1951).

Page 39:   Invitation to ceremonies celebrating the opening of the Golden Gate Bridge (1937).

Page 54:   Fill-in invitation issued by the Eisenhower White House.

Page 54:   Fill-in invitation issued by the Reagan White House.

Page 159: Christmas card sent by the President and Mrs. Roosevelt (1942).

Page 175: Sympathy acknowledgment sent following the death of Pope Pius XI (1939).

Page 188: Invitation to an exhibit by the Bell Telephone Company.

ABOUT THE AUTHOR

Steven L. Feinberg coordinates training and customer development for Crane and Company, Inc., and travels extensively throughout the country giving seminars on the uses of stationery to Crane's clients. He lives in Dalton, Massachusetts.